TA[illegible] ALENT

THE AGE FACTOR AND GENERATION ISSUES

Emma Parry

Peter Urwin

The Chartered Institute of Personnel and Development is the leading publisher of books and reports for personnel and training professionals, students, and all those concerned with the effective management and development of people at work.

For full details of all our titles, please contact the Publishing Department:

Tel: 020 8612 6204

Email: publish@cipd.co.uk

To view and purchase all CIPD titles:

www.cipd.co.uk

For details of CIPD research projects:

www.cipd.co.uk/research

TAPPING INTO TALENT

THE AGE FACTOR AND GENERATION ISSUES

Emma Parry

Peter Urwin

First published 2009

Cover and text design by Sutchinda Rangsi-Thompson

Typeset by Columns Design Ltd, Reading
Printed in Great Britain by Short Run Press, Exeter

British Library Cataloguing in Publication Data
A catalogue record for this book is available from the British Library

ISBN-978-1-84398-240-1

Chartered Institute of Personnel and Development

151 The Broadway, London SW19 1JQ

Tel: 020 8612 6200

Website: www.cipd.co.uk

Incorporated by Royal Charter. Registered charity no. 1079797.

CONTENTS

ACKNOWLEDGEMENTS

The authors would like to thank their colleagues at Cranfield School of Management and Westminster Business School for their help with conducting this literature review.

This report utilises data from the 2007 Labour Force Survey (LFS). The LFS is distributed by the Economic and Social Data Service; Crown Copyright material is reproduced with the permission of the Controller of HMSO and the Queen's Printer for Scotland.

FOREWORD

Talent management was top of the list of business concerns before the world economy took a nosedive. And we should not forget the lessons learned from previous recessions that the underlying skill shortages and demographic changes will come back to bite us on the upturn from the prevailing problems. But while organisations strive to survive the turbulence caused by the financial crisis the more savvy among them know it is imperative to have the best people to navigate themselves out of difficulty and morph into economically viable concerns.

At the same time as some organisations are experiencing business shrinkage, others are finding themselves on an upward surge. And, entrepreneurs are grabbing emerging opportunities for different kinds of business. The economic crisis is triggering business opportunities as well as business disasters and the business community needs to be alert to these to maintain and create new markets. The credit crunch circumstances we face are forcing organisations to make sure their people are their most important asset.

Recent CIPD evidence published in *The War for Talent* report early in 2009 evidences that this is the case because it shows that talent management is reported to be more, not less, important in a recession. Those organisations experiencing recruitment freezes are putting increased effort into developing and using the skills of their existing employees as a way of responding to the challenges they face.

It is clear that excellence in talent management will be vital if organisations are to pull out of the economic downturn. This will make big demands on HR departments to keep on their toes to deliver excellence as a business partner. So how can this new CIPD research report help them do this?

The important findings draw attention to generation and age factors that give important new insights into the ways in which employers can be far more effective in their talent management strategies if they take into account the different needs, preferences and expectations people have about work beyond just having a job.

While many employers have been aware for some time that traditional employment policies and practices don't easily address the expectations of demanding Generation Y employees, neither – as this new evidence shows – would it seem do they always resonate with those of older generations. A 'one size fits all' approach to employment offerings does not hit the mark for the diverse labour market. The upshot of the research is that paying attention to people as individuals and managing diversity is vitally important. This has long been promoted and evidenced by the CIPD in the work it has carried out on managing diversity. By being smarter at managing diversity, organisations will be more likely to tap into the discretionary effort needed from the workforces they depend on.

Employers are hungry for ideas, creativity, ingenuity and innovation to regenerate business success. Awareness and understanding about generational and age factors and how to avoid the bear traps they present will give organisations a leading edge over competitors.

This research report and earlier joint CIPD/Penna survey research, *Gen Up*, give us a much better way to design talent strategies fit for the challenges of the twenty-first century.

Dianah Worman OBE Chartered FCIPD
Adviser, Diversity
Chartered Institute of Personnel and Development

EXECUTIVE SUMMARY

This report summarises the findings of an extensive literature review conducted on behalf of the Chartered Institute of Personnel and Development (CIPD) on the impact of generational diversity on people management. The report focuses on the proposed differences between generations, the validity of these differences and their potential impact on people management.

Overall we can conclude that there are areas of both similarity and difference between individuals from the different generational cohorts. The overwhelming message from this research is that employees should be treated as individuals as much as possible and people management practices should be designed to satisfy a variety of employee needs.

More specifically, the results of this literature review suggest:

- **Generational differences are those that exist between cohorts of individuals born between certain years.** This is proposed to be different from age diversity.
- **It is assumed that there are four generations in the workforce – Veterans, Baby Boomers, Generation X and Generation Y**. These generations are proposed to have different values and characteristics based upon their different life experiences.
- **However, much of the evidence for generational differences is anecdotal and may be due to life stage or age rather than generation;** many practitioners suggest that differences between generations are self-evident.
- **Distinguishing between four generations does not seem necessary in a variety of settings.** For instance, since the 1980s there have been additional skills required for most jobs as a result of technological progress; the key distinction here is between those who entered the labour market before or after this technological shock.
- **In all of the areas where we recognise a potential for generational difference, it is possible that age is the driving force.** For instance, the focus of older generations on pensions as a reward is not surprising and is likely to be driven by considerations of *age*, rather than *generational*, difference.
- **In many areas of the employment relationship where generation is seen to be driving differences, there are other characteristics that are likely to be much more important.** For instance, when we consider flexibility of working, gender remains the key determinant of working patterns and preferences.
- **The cut-off points for the generations in the UK is likely to be different from those proposed for generations in the US.** Generally there is a lag of five to ten years between the US and UK generations.

Despite limitations of the existing evidence base, there are some cross-cutting conclusions that arise from consideration of these proposed differences in generational diversity:

- **Employers must find ways to attract potential employees from across generations.** To do this, they must note that different generations use different recruitment channels and may be attracted by different employer brands.
- **Different generations may have different preferences towards training.** Generations X and Y place great emphasis on development generally and prefer to learn independently, often using computer-based training or the Internet. Baby Boomers and Veterans prefer more traditional classroom or paper-based training.
- **There may be generational differences in employees' attitudes towards careers.** Veterans and Baby Boomers tend to believe that a job is for life whereas Generations X and Y see a job as a way to develop marketable skills and may change careers more frequently.
- **Employers should consider generational differences in preferences for performance management styles.** Baby Boomers like to receive recognition for the hours that they work as well as for

performance, whereas Generations X and Y need immediate and frequent feedback.

- **Money motivates all four generations but they may value other rewards differently.** For instance, Generations X and Y place particular emphasis on work–life balance, whereas retirement and pension provision is of particular importance to Baby Boomers.
- **It has been suggested that flexible working is more important to the younger generations.** However, research has shown that the desire to work flexibly may also increase as employees get nearer to retirement age.
- **The different generations might prefer to be managed in different ways.** Generation X may prefer to be trusted to work independently to authoritarian leadership; Generation Y may wish to have fun and be offered social opportunities; while Baby Boomers and Veterans may focus more on a desire for their experience to be acknowledged.
- **There is potential for the generation gap to lead to conflict within the workplace.** It is possible for stereotypes to develop in the workplace, with Baby Boomers possibly viewing Generation X as 'slackers' and Generation X seeing Baby Boomers as overcautious. This can be overcome through communication and playing to the values and experience of each generation.
- **Finally, it is important to place within context the *overwhelming message that employees should be treated as individuals*, mentioned at the start of this report.** Consideration of diversity across a variety of characteristics is an important component of policies and practices that support the attainment of this goal. However, in considering diversity, we group people according to certain characteristics. It is important to recognise the potential danger that this approach can result in categorising or even stereotyping and we feel that some of the generational literature risks straying into such territory.
- **We must be careful that any proposed differences between generations are not used in a way that legitimises forms of discriminatory thinking, for instance on age.**

LIST OF ABBREVIATIONS AND ACRONYMS

ATM	automated teller machine
BERR	Department of Business, Enterprise and Regulatory Reform
BSAS	British Social Attitudes Survey
CIPD	Chartered Institute of Personnel and Development
DB	defined-benefit pension plans
DC	defined-contribution pension plans
GDP	gross domestic product
HRD	human resource development
ICT	information and communications technologies
laissez-faire	economic approach that emphasises the use of free markets
LFS	Labour Force Survey
OECD	Organisation for Economic Co-operation and Development
SHRM	Society for Human Resource Management
SPA	state pension age

THE IMPORTANCE OF CONSIDERING GENERATIONAL DIVERSITY 1

- **Having a diverse workforce can lead to business benefits such as access to a wider consumer base, satisfying the requirements of public procurement and reaching a wider labour market to address skills shortages.**
- **Generational difference refers to the differences between cohorts of people born between certain years that have similar life experiences, as opposed to age diversity *per se*.**
- **Having a generationally diverse workforce may lead to a range of both positive and negative effects for employers.**

It is generally agreed that diversity in the workplace can lead to a number of business benefits (DTI 2004; Subeliani and Tsogas 2005; Urwin, Michielsens and Waters 2006). There are perceived to be three main areas where employers may expect to see some benefit from the effective promotion and management of diverse workplaces (White et al 2004; Urwin, Michielsens and Waters 2006):

1. A diverse workforce may give firms an advantage in tapping into an increasingly diverse consumer base (in some parts of the literature this is suggested to manifest as a benefit to innovation).
2. There is the case of firms that are engaged in competition for contracts as part of the process of public procurement (where diversity requirements are often placed within the terms of the contracts).
3. The main reason why firms became interested in the promotion of diversity was in response to skills shortages in the recent period of tight labour markets (White et al 2004; Urwin, Michielsens and Waters 2006) because it may allow employers access to a wider range of potential employees.

The CIPD, in its recent publication *Managing Diversity and the Business Case* (2008c), listed eight possible components of the business case for diversity:

- customer care and marketplace competitiveness
- corporate image, brand, ethics and values
- recruitment and retention of talent
- designing and delivering products and services
- increasing creativity and innovation
- being an employer of choice through effective people management and development
- complying with legislation
- corporate social responsibility.

Research from the CIPD (2008c) (conducted in 2007 but covered in the same report) showed that the most important of these, according to survey respondents, was recruiting and retaining talent (64%).

There are many reasons to suggest that the present focus around the management and enhancement of diversity (Litvin 1997; Swann et al 2004; White et al 2004; Foster and Harris 2005) is now embedded in the workings of many firms and will continue into the present downturn. While the original motivation for many firms' focus on diversity was a response to the perceived problem of skills shortages (see, for instance, CIPD 2002), the pace of globalisation and the rise of the truly multinational firm have acted as further catalysts. As a recent report (Michielsens, Bingham and Clarke 2008) underlines:

> *The business arguments focus not only on optimising talent resources, but also on optimising client attraction, reducing costs and stimulating innovation. The increasing global importance of diversity in the tendering process makes it a crucial element in gaining contracts.*

The diversity literature tends to focus on those aspects of 'difference' where there is some aspect of legislation. That is, gender, ethnicity, disability, religion, age and sexual orientation. However, the focus of many company policies and therefore the majority of academic studies tends to be on gender and ethnicity. More recently, due to the recent UK legislation on age, interest in age diversity has also increased.

GENERATIONAL DIVERSITY

Work on generational diversity assumes that the differing experiences of certain age groups lead to similarities within, and significant differences between, generations in their behaviours and expectations. As with other dimensions of diversity, alerting employers and policy-makers to any generational 'difference' is an essential first step. If there is evidence that generations do exhibit differences that cut across other socioeconomic groupings (such as gender, ethnicity, religion, social class, and so on), then taking these into account will better ensure policies and practices that promote inclusion. Going further than this, the creation of such an inclusive environment may allow us to manage generational diversity in a way that improves business performance, rather than simply attempting to avoid conflict.

Recent survey results from the Society for Human Resource Management (SHRM) provide some insight into when generational differences may play a role within organisations (see Table 1). This research of over 250 HR managers suggests that generational diversity within an organisation can have both positive and negative effects.

Table 1: Occurrence of events where generational differences are perceived to play a role (%) (Burke 2004)

	Frequently	Occasionally	Rarely	Never
workers from different generations working effectively together	51	46	3	0
workers from different generations learning from one another	31	55	15	0
better quality of work due to variety of generational perspectives	27	55	15	3
conflicts regarding acceptable work hours between workers of different generations	24	42	29	5
employees feeling co-workers from other generations do not respect them	20	45	30	6
communication breakdowns between workers of different generations	19	57	22	2
intergenerational mentoring (formal or informal)	16	41	35	8
perspectives of workers from two or more different generations balancing one another	14	54	29	3
employees stating that co-workers from other generations are over- or under-reliant on technology	14	45	33	8
employees taking co-workers from other generations less seriously	13	47	33	8
resentment between workers of different generations	8	29	45	18

The purpose of this report is to consider what is known about generational diversity and its impact on people management through a review of the academic and practitioner literature in this area. Chapter 2 of the report begins the process of review by setting out the research into generations that has involved defining cut-off points among the present age distribution of populations (usually in post-industrial Western countries) and ascribing characteristics to each (Taylor 2005; Glass 2007). As we shall see, the differences in characteristics, mainly behaviours and expectations, are usually ascribed as a result of shared experiences within cohorts of individuals.

However, as Chapter 3 underlines, there has only been a limited amount of research conducted into generational differences, especially in the UK. Therefore, a critical review is needed, as some of the claims made for 'difference' seem to be based on anecdote, rather than robust evidence. Before providing advice to employers we need to ensure the validity and usefulness of the distinctions that are often made between various age groups to specify generations. Having carried out this review of the existing evidence, the remainder of the report focuses on discussion in the main areas of HR management practice. In each of these areas of investigation we consider the claims that have been made for generational diversity and the implications for employer policies to promote inclusion and capture any business benefits.

In this report we spread the net wide and consider all of the major areas of the employment relationship where issues of generational diversity may arise:

- Chapter 4 begins by considering the area that has formed the focus of diversity, *recruitment and selection*.
- Chapter 5 considers the possibility of different views across generations with respect to *training and development.*
- Chapter 6 considers generational differences for *career development and performance*.
- Chapter 7 examines *rewards and working patterns.*

In these chapters of the report there is some consideration of the interactions between individuals of different generations; for instance, work-based, on-the-job training tends to involve more experienced workers passing on their skills to those at an earlier stage in their career. When we come to the final two chapters, this interaction becomes a focus of our attention. In the latter sections of the report we are particularly cautious in considering the claims that have been made for the differences between generations, as we are less able to draw on the more extensive work that has age as its focus. These last two chapters are:

- Chapter 8: Management style and leadership
- Chapter 9: Avoiding generational or age 'conflict'.

GENERATIONAL VERSUS AGE DIVERSITY

Given that we will refer to both the 'age' and 'generational' literatures, it is important to distinguish between these two aspects of the diversity debate. Thus, for the purposes of this report, **generational difference** can be seen as arising from the differing experiences of groups of individuals, as they experience differing social (and economic) conditions from those of earlier or later generations *at the same age*. The implication is that, at the same point in their working lives, these differing experiences will lead to different behaviours and preferences. As an example, one can imagine a number of differences we could identify between the behaviours and experiences of those aged 28–43 between 1974 and 1992 (Baby Boomers) and the same age group between 1993 and the present day (Generation X). Such differences would be distinct from age effects, but the reality is that we only observe Baby Boomers and Generation X at the present time when any generational effects are hard to distinguish from any age-related differences.

Thus, in addition to the proposed differences between generations we may reasonably expect there to be differences in the preferences and behaviours of people from **different age groups**. For instance, we may expect more of a focus on the pension aspects of reward as people age; while in early career there may be more concern over the opportunities for acquisition of skills, no matter what generation we are considering. In reality, we observe a variety of different generations among the present population and it is quite possible that any of the differences in behaviours and preferences being ascribed to these could simply be about age. This means that we need to make sure that we distinguish questions of generational diversity from ones that ask, 'what are the differences in preferences and behaviours as we age?'

This is a simplistic approach to the issue of age and generational difference, as it is quite possible that the two may interact to such an extent that the ageing process itself is fundamentally changed as a result of generational experience. However, it is still a useful distinction to make in some areas of our discussion because it provides an indication of whether any generational differences are likely to be more or less short-lived.

THE GENERATIONS AND THEIR PROPOSED DIFFERENCES

2

- **There are currently assumed to be four generations in the workforce – Veterans, Baby Boomers, Generation X and Generation Y.**
- **Each generation has been proposed to have specific characteristics and values that make it different from other generations, regardless of age.**
- **These differences in characteristics are said to be caused by each generation's life experiences, such as the state of the economy and labour market, family values and political events while they were growing up.**
- **We should not presume that the characteristics of generational cohorts within the UK are the same as those that have been widely documented in the US.**

To understand the impact of generational differences within the workplace, and the potential implications of this for people management, we first need to understand the nature of the generations that have been suggested to exist and the supposed characteristics of each. We can then carry out a critical review of the claims made for any generational difference by considering the theory and evidence. This chapter sets out age groupings for the generations and the claims made for them. Chapter 3 then considers the validity of these claims and, as we shall see, the evidence presented here needs to come with a 'health warning' because a lot of the claims made in the existing literature have a weak evidence base.

It is generally accepted that there are currently four generations within the workforce. These are Veterans, Baby Boomers, Generation X and Generation Y. There is some disagreement in the literature about the exact years in which these groups were born, but for the sake of this report, we will use the definitions set out in Table 2 (taken from Jenkins 2008).

Table 2: Generations and their importance to population and employment

Generation	Born	Age in 2008	Proportion of UK population	Proportion of total UK employed	Also known as
Veterans	1925–1945	63–83	16%	9%	Matures The Silent Generation Traditionalists
Baby Boomers	1946–1964	44–62	25%	36%	
Generation X	1965–1980	28–43	23%	35%	Baby Busters 13th Generation/ Thirteeners The Lost Generation
Generation Y	1981 onwards	27 or less	36%	20%	Nexters Echo Boomers Millennials
Total frequency			59 million	36 million	

Source: Data are taken from *Labour Force Survey*, 2007, and categories from Jenkins (2008).

Past attention has mainly focused on the proposed characteristics of the demographic groups that make up Generation X and the Baby Boomers because their values and preferences at work are likely to dominate, given that they make up over 70% of those in employment. Given that the age of 65 still represents the point of retirement for many workers, it is not surprising to see that Veterans constitute less than 10% of those in employment. Finally, the importance of those from Generation Y in the workforce is already quite substantial and will grow over the next few years; interestingly, however, it is not likely to reach the proportionate importance of other generations due to the fall in birth rates over recent decades and the subsequent ageing of the population.

As we detail later in the report, much of the literature on generational diversity has come from the US. Recent research by the US Society for Human Resource Management (Burke 2004) asked respondents what percentage of the workforce at their current location was in each generation. On average, the largest proportion of the workforce was Baby Boomers, followed by Generation X (see Figure 1). While the two sources are not directly comparable for a number of reasons, there would seem to be some correspondence between the UK and US figures (with the higher proportion of Baby Boomers and lower figure for Generation Y reflecting the earlier period at which the figures were constructed for the US).

Figure 1 ✣ Proportion of US workforce in each generation

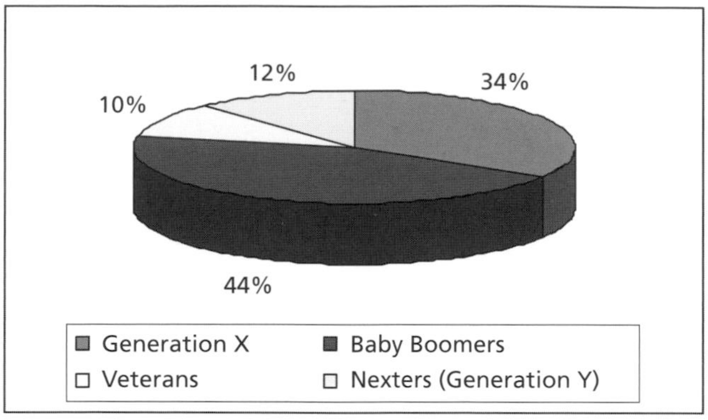

12%
34%
10%
44%

Generation X
Baby Boomers
Veterans
Nexters (Generation Y)

Source: Burke 2004

PROPOSED CHARACTERISTICS OF GENERATIONS

As we can see, considering both employment and careers in the UK and US, these cohorts are at very different stages in their lives. Most Veterans have already retired, while many Baby Boomers are reaching the end of their working lives and considering retirement. Generation X has now been in the workforce for between 10 and 30 years, while Generation Y is just entering the workforce. It is perhaps not surprising that they have been ascribed different preferences and attributes. We will discuss the debate on whether (and why) these groups are actually different in the next chapter, but first, let us look at the attributes that have been suggested for each generation.

Veterans

Veterans are generally characterised as being loyal to employers, believing in hard work, believing in the status quo and having respect for authority figures. Veterans believe in the intrinsic value of hard work and have a work ethic that hinges on loyalty, dependability and a 'stick to it' mentality. They obtain job satisfaction from the work itself and from doing a job well and do not necessarily need the work to have particular meaning (Berl 2006).

Zemke, Raines and Filipczak (2000) describe the core values of veterans as:

- dedication/sacrifice
- hard work
- conformity
- law and order
- respect for authority
- patience
- delayed reward
- duty before pleasure
- adherence to rules
- honour.

On the job they are seen as:

- stable
- detail-oriented
- thorough
- loyal
- hard-working
- inept with ambiguity and change
- reluctant to buck the system
- uncomfortable with conflict
- reticent when they disagree.

Baby Boomers

Baby Boomers' core values have been described as optimism, team orientation, personal gratification, health and wellness, personal growth and an obsession with youth, work and involvement. They place emphasis on a sense of accomplishment, achievement and social recognition. They are dedicated; in fact they might be seen as workaholics and are willing to put in long hours and use their personal resources to get the job done. They regularly work 50–60 hours per week (Berl 2006; Carlson 2004). Baby Boomers place a higher value on work itself than the later generations and receive higher levels of job satisfaction in general. They value warm, friendly relationships with co-workers (Jurkewicz and Brown 1998).

Zemke, Raines and Filipczak (2000) describe the core values of Baby Boomers as:

- optimism
- team orientation
- personal gratification
- health and wellness
- personal growth
- youth
- work
- involvement.

On the job they are seen as:

- service-oriented
- driven
- willing to 'go the extra mile'
- good at relationships
- wanting to please
- good team players
- not naturally budget-minded
- uncomfortable with conflict
- reluctant to go against peers
- sometimes putting process ahead of result
- overly sensitive to feedback
- judgemental of those who see things differently
- self-centred.

Generation X

Much of the literature on Generation X underlines our need to be cautious in interpretations because there is a stereotyping of this group as getting bored quickly, having a short attention span, expecting immediate gratification and distrusting institutions (Filipczak 1994; Caudron 1997). Tulgan (1996) noted that some commentators also suggest that they have been perceived as lazy, disloyal and arrogant, but research has shown that they are actually self-reliant rather than arrogant, adaptable to change rather than disloyal and prefer to learn by assimilating information from multiple sources. Generation X values a sense of belonging and teamwork, the ability to learn new things, autonomy and entrepreneurship, security and flexibility. They tend to be sceptical of the status quo and hierarchical relationships and believe a manager must earn respect rather than deserve it by virtue of their title (Tulgan 1996). They are independent and resourceful, comfortable with diversity, value integrity and expect a balanced lifestyle (Bova and Kroth 1999).

Zemke, Raines and Filipczak (2000) describe the core values of Generation X as:

- diversity
- thinking globally
- balance
- techno-literacy
- fun
- informality
- self-reliance
- pragmatism.

On the job they are seen as:

- adaptable
- techno-literate
- independent
- not intimidated by authority
- creative
- impatient
- having poor people skills
- inexperienced
- cynical.

Generation Y

Much less is known about the characteristics of Generation Y, probably due to their more recent entry into the labour market. However, this generation is seen as having similar characteristics to Generation X and also as being team-oriented, co-operative and interdependent, and possessing tighter peer bonds (McCafferty 2003). Generation Y is particularly technologically savvy with high personal experience of Web 2.0 technology. Research from the Chartered Institute of Management (Macleod 2008) found that 31% of young managers had read a blog entry in the last few months and 10% had written one themselves. Fifty-six per cent of young managers used Facebook, with this rising to 75% of those under 25.

Zemke, Raines and Filipczak (2000) describe the core values of Generation Y as:

- optimism
- civic duty
- confidence
- achievement
- sociability
- morality
- street smarts
- diversity.

On the job they are seen as being characterised by:

- collective action
- optimism

- tenacity
- heroic spirit
- multitasking capabilities
- technologically savvy
- need for supervision and support
- inexperienced, particularly with handling difficult people issues.

The *proposed* differences between the four generations are summarised in Table 3.

Table 3: Workplace values (taken from Crumpacker and Crumpacker 2007)

	Veteran/Traditionalist	Baby Boomer	Generation X	Generation Y
Dominant values	benevolence loyalty conformity custom	tolerance power/authority achievement stimulation	stimulation self-direction achievement hedonism	stimulation self-direction hedonism
Stereotypes	old-fashioned/rigid autocratic don't want to learn new ways of working	workaholic political self-centred	cynical lazy selfish	spoiled technology-dependent scatterbrained
Work ethic	disciplined duty before play adhere to the rules	efficient logical self-centred	task-oriented self-reliant independent	multitasking group-oriented explain why
Communication	formal written chain of command	face time one-on-one in person	direct as needed	email/ voice mail instant messaging lots of CCs
Feedback	avoid conflict no news is good news	'show me the money' promotion/title	direct – 'tell me how I am doing'	instantaneous seek approval/praise
Leadership	command and control take charge authoritative	collaborative team player	entrepreneurial participative wants to know why	n/a
Authority	follow authority figure hierarchical chain of command	question authority	sceptical of authority	lines are blurred why must I follow?
Family and work	family and work are always separate	work takes priority over all else	work–life balance	work–life balance if must choose will select family and friends

	Veteran/Traditionalist	Baby Boomer	Generation X	Generation Y
Rewards	appreciate recognition for a job well done opportunity to mentor	appreciate promotion, title, money opportunity to build consensus	appreciate autonomy and flexibility	appreciate opportunity to provide input technical wiz

Survey research from the Society for Human Resource Management (Burke 2004) has provided some empirical support for the workplace traits attributed to each generation. Respondents to this research most commonly ascribed the following characteristics to each generational cohort.

Veterans

- plan to stay with the organisation over the long term
- respectful of organisational hierarchy
- like structure
- accepting of authority figures in the workplace
- give maximum effort

Baby Boomers

- give maximum effort
- accepting of authority figures in the workplace
- results-driven
- plan to stay with the organisation over the long term
- retain what they learn

Generation X

- technologically savvy
- like informality
- learn quickly
- seek work–life balance
- embrace diversity

Generation Y

- technologically savvy
- like informality
- embrace diversity
- learn quickly
- need supervision

It can be seen from the above list that Veterans and Baby Boomers are relatively similar in their traits, but there is then a shift in the characteristics from these generations to Generations X and Y, who also seem relatively similar. This begs the question as to whether it is valid to actually divide the workforce into only two generations rather than four. This will be discussed further later in this report.

The CIPD recently (May–July 2008) joined with Penna to conduct research examining the strategic implications for attracting, managing and retaining the four generations of Veterans, Baby Boomers, Generation X and Generation Y. This research took the form of an online survey of over 5,500 employees from organisations across industry sectors, organisation sizes, generations, management grades and pay grades, across six Western European countries, including the UK. The research also included focus groups and interviews with senior HR managers from UK organisations to explore the challenges they face as employers and the practical actions taken to address generational differences.

Throughout this report, we include findings from the CIPD/Penna research where the findings are relevant to our discussion. The full CIPD/Penna report, *Gen Up*, can be obtained from **www.penna.com**

PROPOSED CAUSES OF GENERATIONAL CHARACTERISTICS

What drives these supposed differences in the behaviours and expectations of generations? Each generation is believed to have been shaped by its experiences and by the experiences of their parents, so the generations are different because they have lived through different experiences while growing up. For instance, Generation X entered into the labour market in the 1980s and early 1990s without any expectations of job security. They saw their parents being made redundant and this shaped their perceptions of work in a time of economic uncertainty. This has been seen to lead to a tendency to see every job as temporary and each company as a 'stepping stone' to something else (Filipczak 1994). Many individuals from Generation X were 'latchkey kids', viewed as resenting the amount of time that their parents spent at work and therefore growing up to be self-reliant and independent problem-solvers.

Having grown up with computers at home, they are assumed to be techno-literate and are used to ATMs and microwave ovens so expect immediate gratification and to receive answers and feedback immediately (Caudron 1997), though they can remember a period before the ubiquity of the Internet. In addition, about 40% of this cohort grew up in single-parent families and the assumption is that they are more determined to spend time with their families (Bova and Kroth 1999). In contrast to Generation X, Veterans grew up during the Depression so grew up believing in hard work and being loyal to employers in return for employment, and Baby Boomers grew up against the background of the 'American Dream', believing that they would be rewarded for hard work and long hours.

The following summarises some of the possible events that might be considered as 'drivers' of difference for US generational cohorts. As suggested previously, much of the interest in generational difference has come from the US and it is therefore important to consider the transferability of this framework to UK generational cohorts.

Traditionalists, or Veterans

- Great Depression
- New Deal
- Second World War
- Korean War

Baby Boomers

- civil rights
- sexual revolution
- Cold War
- space travel
- assassinations

Generation X

- fall of Berlin Wall
- Watergate
- women's liberation
- Desert Storm
- energy crisis

Generation Y

- school shootings
- Oklahoma City
- technology
- child-focused world
- Clinton/Lewinsky

There are clearly some experiences that will have been shared across the Atlantic, such as the fall of the Berlin Wall, women's liberation and the technological revolution. However, we need to supplement the existing research base by providing some additional background information on the nature of the economic and social environments for generations within the UK. So what are some of the broad historical trends in the UK that we might wish to consider as factors that have shaped the characteristics of each of the four generations?

GENERATIONAL EXPERIENCES IN THE UK

We consider the events that will have been experienced by each generation during their formative years.

Veterans

The Great Depression of the 1930s is assumed to have started with the Wall Street Crash of 1929, but economic conditions had already begun to decline before that. In the 1920s unemployment had remained high at around 10% and rose to 30% in the 1930s.

This point in history caused a wholesale change in the political, social and economic consensus of the time. Prior to the 1930s, governments adhered to a view of the world that had limited their interventions in the economy and society. The first UK Labour Government, under Ramsay McDonald, had only been in power between January and November 1924. This was a world in which social and economic justice, as reflected by a social 'safety net', had yet to take hold as a political consensus.

This *laissez-faire* consensus changed dramatically between the Depression of the 1930s and the period after the First World War, when the return of nearly 3 million men from military service coincided with a sharp downturn in economic activity. Policy-makers came under increasing pressure to intervene. It is during this period of changing consensus that the Veterans became economically, socially and politically active – according to our cut-off points, they will have been 16 between 1941 and 1961.

While one would not want to discount the terrible loss of life during the Second World War and the initial years of reconstruction, the essential experience during this period for the majority of Veterans was (a) growing stability and prosperity (though from a relatively impoverished situation following the Second World War), and (b) the growth of the welfare state and a new political consensus that saw an important role for governments in the economy. This new 'post-war' consensus lasted up to the mid-1970s.

Baby Boomers

From the end of the Second World War up to the 1970s, governments adopted what were called 'Keynesian' approaches to the economy, with a deliberate managing of demand to smooth out the economic cycle. This approach to economic policy reflected a greater involvement of successive UK governments in many areas of life where there was felt to be a potential impact on the social welfare of the population (for instance, the growing welfare state and industrial relations policy). 'Post-war consensus' is a term that describes the high degree of agreement between the political parties.

During the 1950s and 1960s this approach seemed to work well, and though the UK went through a period of 'relative' decline, inflation in the UK averaged just 3.8% and unemployment a mere 1.7%. From an economic perspective it would seem reasonable to suggest that the early Baby Boomers, who entered the labour market (that is, became 16) between 1962 and 1980, would have had a similar experience to the Veterans.

However, when we consider social change over this post-war period, then we may reasonably expect there to be a difference in the experience of Veterans and Baby Boomers because the latter were becoming 16 throughout the 1960s and 1970s. There has been a lot written about the 1960s and it is often focused primarily on the US, for instance in terms of the anti-war movement. Many of these phenomena did not translate over to the UK for a number of years (for instance the Stonewall riots of 1969), or can be seen as impacting more on the way that UK society perceived the US, rather than UK society itself (the assassinations are a case in point).

However, it is safe to say that during the 1960s and 1970s in the UK there was something of a 'sexual' revolution, arising from both the introduction of the pill in 1960 and other social trends that gave women more economic and social independence. This was accompanied by a growing awareness of wider 'equality' issues, with respect to ethnicity and sexual orientation. These trends between the 1950s and 1970s are closely intertwined with the rise of consumer society when young men and women will have had some of the first experiences of disposable income.

Generation X

By the end of the 1970s the post-war consensus had begun to break down and the two main political parties were beginning to propose divergent economic and social policies with which to solve the problems of the British economy. The oil shocks of 1974 and 1979 resulted in 'stagflation' (a situation where there is both high unemployment and inflation) and economists such as Milton Friedman were suggesting alternatives to Keynesian economics. Following the 'winter of discontent' in 1979, the Conservative Government of Margaret Thatcher was elected to power on a radical agenda that adopted many of the monetarist ideas put forward by Friedman.

Though the Conservatives' love affair with the monetarism of Friedman did not last long, their focus on supply-side economics and the deregulation of markets continued throughout the 1980s. The basic ideas were very similar to those put forward prior to the 1930s and the suggestion was that the problems of the British economy resulted from too much government intervention and control in the economy. Again this economic view is reflected in a changing social view; where the post-war consensus saw a role for government in the economy that spilled over into a growing social role, the new view was more associated with individualism, rather than community (though Margaret Thatcher's famous quote that 'there is no such thing' as society is not as it seems).

This period of change and upheaval was the backdrop to labour market entry for those of Generation X, who became 16 between 1981 and 1996, before the start of the decade-long boom that has recently ended.

During the 1980s the Thatcher Government introduced legislation to curb trade union power; foreign exchange controls were lifted; the standard rate of income tax was cut from 33% to 30% (with VAT being raised to compensate for the loss of revenue); loss-making nationalised industries were privatised and restrictive employment practices were abolished. A major aim of government policy was to reduce government spending (as a proportion of GDP) and tight monetary policy was backed up by tight fiscal policy. In the public mind, the government's policy became synonymous with cuts.

Though these policies are now seen to have been necessary, they were vigorously opposed by many in the UK during the 1980s and this resulted in severe social unrest, which often took the form of violent protest. In contrast to previous governments, during the 1980s the Conservatives did not believe in protecting the jobs of those who worked in industries such as mining and steel manufacture and, as a result of the industrial restructuring that this approach implied, unemployment reached 3.1 million in 1986. This led to massive social unrest, including the miners strike, which began in 1984, and the poll tax riots in the summer of 1990, riots that made a significant contribution to Margaret Thatcher's removal from power in 1990.

Generation Y

Margaret Thatcher resigned in November 1990 and was succeeded as party leader and prime minister by John Major, who went on to win the 1992 general election by a narrow margin. When John Major became prime minister any economic stability was still a long way off. On 'Black Wednesday' (16 September 1992), the pound was forced out of the Exchange Rate Mechanism by a group of international speculators led by the Hungarian-born US fund manager George Soros.

However, this marked a turning point and Prime Minister John Major oversaw the beginnings of a long period of recovery and falling rates of unemployment. It was also the starting point for a new consensus, as the Labour Party under Neil Kinnock began to move the party from the left of the political spectrum towards the centre ground. As a first step, the infamous 'Clause 4' was scrapped from the Labour Party's manifesto, which until then had committed the party to the nationalisation of key industries.

The reformed Labour Party won a landslide victory at the general election in 1997. The faith in the rebranded 'new' Labour Party and a string of political scandals just before the general election in 1997 had spelled the end of Conservative government after 18 years in power. Despite its commitment to low taxes, Prime Minister Tony Blair made it clear that the health and education sectors would see significant increases in government spending. This was made possible by a growing economy with one of the lowest levels of unemployment in Europe. The increasing tax base enabled Chancellor Gordon Brown to set aside extra money for the National Health Service and schools in six consecutive budgets without having to significantly increase the tax burden for UK citizens.

Clearly this latter period of prosperity from around the mid-1990s until 2007 has been the main backdrop to the experiences of Generation Y as they became 16 years old from 1997 onwards. In many ways, we can view the differences between Generation X and those from Generation Y as being the former's experience of both the depths of bust and the heights of boom (in contrast to the post-war years until the 1970s when the Baby Boomers and Veterans experienced fewer extremes); compared with a Generation Y that has only known prosperity and full employment (apart from a minor dip at the end of the 1990s and beginning of 2000s). However, this is no longer the case and the present severe downturn is likely to work to align the experiences of these two younger generations.

THE IMPACT OF TECHNOLOGY

In addition to this changing environment, perhaps the most substantial change has been the introduction of computers in the workplace and more generally the revolution in information and communications technology (ICT). Clearly this has had an impact on Generation Y to a greater extent, as they have less knowledge of a world where ICTs are not ubiquitous. However, both Generations X and Y have grown up in a world where these technologies have been increasingly used, while Baby Boomers have had to deal with the introduction of technology. We could therefore question the extent to which a significant distinction can be made between Generations X and Y on this dimension, although it might be suggested that Generation X has been influenced mainly by IT whereas Generation Y could be called the 'Internet' generation.

The above discussion has underlined how the research on experiences of generations in the US cannot simply be mapped onto experiences within the UK. Some of the reasons why this is the case are, for instance, the fact that the post-war consensus in the UK is closely entwined with the introduction and expansion of the welfare state. However, the main difference is the fact that during the period between the 1930s and 1970s the UK suffered a period of relative decline, with most other countries of the world catching up and overtaking the UK (in terms of both economic and political influence). In contrast, the US experienced growing influence on the world stage (though events such as the Vietnam War have not made this a smooth path) and after the 1980s was confirmed as the only superpower. In many ways Generation X and Y have entered working life during periods when the UK's relative decline has been seen to be reversed.

In fact, we may reasonably expect the UK to define its generations in a way that is similar to the US, but 'lagged' by something between five and ten years. Thus, the introduction of the Race Relations Act 1965 in the UK was 11 years after *Brown vs. Board of Education* in the US in 1954. Following the Stonewall riots in 1969, the Gay Liberation Front held its first UK conference in 1972. More importantly, for the study here, in the US there has been an age discrimination act since 1967 and within the UK it would seem reasonable to suggest that the X and Y generations have grown up with a more pronounced conceptualisation of discrimination, and more recently diversity, than was previously the case. As we consider later, an understanding of diversity and age discrimination itself may have an impact on the interactions between generations.

The idea that different events in the UK and US have led to generational differences in these two countries begs the question of whether generational characteristics are the same across countries. If generational differences are based on common life events then one may propose that the generations across western Europe at least will have similar characteristics. However, one may also expect that, in other countries such as Japan or China, the nature of generational cohorts and their characteristics may be very different. In addition, the impact of national culture should not be forgotten. While western European individuals of a similar age may have experienced similar events through the world wars, economic cycles and technological revolution, they will have entered the workforce under very different working environments. Authors such as Hofstede have demonstrated that countries across Europe have very different national cultures due to the regulatory and economic environment and this will have an impact on people's values and expectations in the workplace. This is something that should be considered when discussing generational diversity, particularly in light of the increasingly multinational nature of the workforce.

ARE THE GENERATIONS SO DIFFERENT? 3

- **Many of the differences between generations appear self-evident but much of the evidence for these differences is anecdotal.**
- **Some of the differences between generations can be explained in relation to age or life stage.**
- **Generational differences may exist but may still be less important to employers than other differences, such as gender.**

In the last chapter we discussed generational differences as though the definitions of each generation and their characteristics were widely accepted. We must recognise however that there is some debate about whether these differences actually exist and to what extent they are substantial enough to warrant consideration in addition to the many existing characteristics of diversity. In this chapter we attempt to shed light on these questions.

The above distinctions between generations are now widely accepted in the United States and are gaining credence in the UK and in other countries. However, the acceptance of these definitions is not universal and some authors have questioned whether the attitudes of individuals really are dependent on when they were born. More accurately, while it might seem reasonable to suggest that shared socioeconomic experiences have resulted in shared generational beliefs/characteristics, there are many dimensions of difference to take into account when considering diversity. The question we need to ask is whether considerations of generational difference are substantial enough to warrant separate consideration.

DO WE REALLY NEED ANOTHER ASPECT OF WORKPLACE DIVERSITY?

Social trends have increased the levels of workplace diversity on a number of dimensions over recent decades. For instance, there are growing numbers of women and ethnic minorities in the workplace and demographic projections continue to predict a rise in the proportion of older individuals in the population. This increasing emphasis on workplace diversity has been accompanied by an increase in focus on the equal opportunities agenda (including age, religion and sexual orientation), and promotions such as the Work–life Balance Campaign or Work–life Balance Challenge Fund (Nelson et al 2004).

One can view all of these 'strands' as different aspects of the policies and practices that relate to *workplace diversity*. We may question therefore whether we really need to add another 'branch' of diversity by studying the possible differences between generations, particularly when it is possible that a lot of what passes for generational differences may actually be more about age diversity. The question for this and the remaining sections of the report therefore is not just whether there are differences between the generations, but also whether any differences are substantial enough to warrant consideration.

ARE THERE GENUINE DIFFERENCES BETWEEN GENERATIONAL COHORTS?

Many readers will consider that the differences between generations are self-evident. As an example, the cohorts born after 1965 (Generations X and Y) are more likely to be IT-literate, other things remaining equal, and this is an important distinction to consider in the design of workplace training. 'Generation' may therefore be seen as a defining characteristic, cutting across gender, ethnicity, disability, and so on when considering training that involves a component of ICT. However, if we consider the desire or otherwise for flexible working arrangements, we may conclude that gender remains the key dimension on which attitudes to flexible working are determined. This does not rule out the possibility that some patterns of preference can be explained by generational groupings. Rather, in this case we may consider them as secondary as they do not cut across gender categories.

Given the extensive literature that has developed around issues of gender, ethnicity and age, any arguments that employers should also take account of generational diversity are weakened by the fact that little solid research has analysed the differences between generations, particularly in the UK. In fact, most of the literature in this area is not academic or empirical. The concept of generational diversity is one that has evolved from a branch of the marketing and advertising literature that seems to have little empirical support. To provide true evidence for differences in generational cohorts, a longitudinal research study would be needed to identify differences between generational cohorts over time. Unfortunately, a study of this type has not, as yet, been performed. A number of snapshots of the differences between generations have been conducted but these are inconclusive. In fact, Jurkiewicz and Brown (1998) found that Baby Boomers and Generation X were more alike than different when asked to rank 15 work-related motivational factors, therefore refuting commonly held assumptions that Generation X and Baby Boomers want different things from their jobs. Similarly, Gonzales (2006) found no differences between Generations X, Y and Baby Boomers in their work ethic.

AGE AND LIFE STAGE DIFFERENCES

It may be that some of the differences espoused as generational differences can be ascribed to age and to life and career stages as opposed to generational cohorts. While personality characteristics may remain stable, people generally change what they want from their jobs over time as they progress from pre-graduate employment to career positions, mix family and career interests, and onto retirement. Individuals' concern for particular personnel benefits shift throughout life depending on the age of the employee.

For instance, Baby Boomers are reported to be concerned with retirement issues while Generation X want childcare and Veterans want secure pensions. These variations in what employees want from their jobs may be viewed inside the context of the employee life cycle – as employees enter the workforce they may favour certain benefits over others and these preferences will change as they get older and as their situation in life changes. This is true of all generations and at similar points in their life cycles (Jurkiewicz 2000). Giancola (2006) also provided a list of doubts regarding generational differences, including the fact that beliefs and attitudes change over the life span and the lack of empirical research in this area.

In fact both generational cohort and life stages might be important in deciding how a person governs their behaviour (Polach 2006). Some behaviour transcends generational values and can better be explained using life stages. Common life stages are:

- **youth** (ages 0–21) – a period of learning and growth
- **rising adulthood** (ages 22–35) – priority placed on establishing career and family and the pressure to balance these needs
- **midlife** (ages 36–50) – characterised by the desire for more leadership opportunities and a fuller desire to parent and mentor plus the pressure to 'have it all'
- **legacy** (ages 50–70) – a period of reaffirming values and a strong pressure to keep what has been earned
- **elderhood** (aged 70 and over) – focused on the 'giving back' and passing on values and methods.

The idea that employees' values and needs change according to life stage was reflected in recent CIPD research into managing an ageing workforce (CIPD 2008b). The results of a focus group of older workers within the cosmetics company Molton Brown showed that workers who were nearing retirement often placed a higher emphasis on flexible working arrangements and social opportunities at work rather than salary. The group explained that they had fewer commitments such as childcare or mortgages than they had earlier in their working lives so wanted to have more time away from work to enjoy their income before retirement. Older workers also enjoyed social opportunities at work, with over a third of respondents to a CIPD survey stating that the reason they would work after retirement age was for social interaction. These findings are in opposition to much of the literature on generational differences that suggests that younger employees from Generation X or Y are more focused on flexible working or social opportunities at work, therefore casting some doubt on the validity of the espoused generational differences.

The importance of differentiating between the two drivers of difference (age and generational differences) is that age effects are generally well known to Western employers, in contrast to any changing considerations of generation. However, as suggested previously, it is a little simplistic to consider these separately and there seems to be some value in combining our understanding of life stages with a generational approach. A combination of approaches provides us with a significantly better understanding of how to leverage age diversity in an increasingly complicated workforce than one that relies solely on generational cohorts alone. Of course, ideally we would treat each employee as an individual with their own specific needs and values. This may not always be practical but some consideration of how employee needs differ by life stage and generation are a step in the right direction.

THE INTERACTION BETWEEN GENERATIONAL DIFFERENCES AND OTHER AREAS OF DIVERSITY

As an example of (a) the interaction between ageing and generational difference and (b) the importance of other aspects of diversity as explanations of difference (in this case gender), it is useful to consider Figure 2, which charts the decline in the proportion of economically active individuals aged 55 to 64, from 1950 onwards. At first glance the data seem to imply that the phenomenon of falling participation at the end of working life is limited to males. However, comparison between the situation of men and women is complicated because it is hard to disentangle any fall in older women's participation from the general upward trend in the participation of women from all age groups. Despite this complication, older women have suffered a relative decline in economic activity, as they have not seen their employment rates rise in line with those of their younger counterparts.

There is an extensive literature investigating the possible reasons why the UK, together with many other countries of the OECD, have witnessed such a dramatic decline in older individuals' economic activity rates (Disney 1999; Taylor and Urwin 1999; Blundell, Meghir and Smith 2002). There would seem to be a general consensus that the large amount of restructuring that many economies have undergone since the mid-1970s – as a result of increased international competition, technological change and deregulation – has had a disproportionate effect on the labour market situation of older individuals. However, since this point there has been some

Figure 2 ✣ Proportion of economically active individuals by age

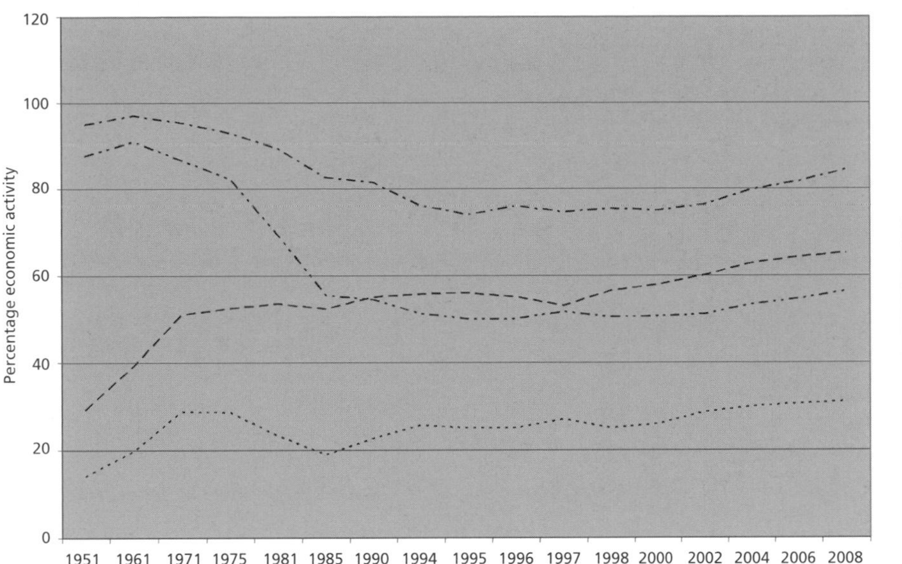

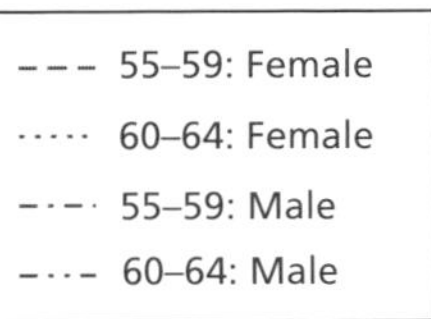

Source: *Employment Gazette*, April 1995, *Labour Force Survey*, Spring 1995–2008

recovery in participation rates. In 2008, 73% of men aged between 50 and 64 were economically active, compared with 70% in 2001. For women the rise in activity for those between 50 and 59 has been from around 65% in 2001 to 70% in 2008.

Figure 2 shows how important gender and age are as explanations of differing experiences across generations and in a reflection of this, most studies of the labour market consider men and women separately, as they still have (on average) very different labour market profiles. However, the term 'on average' is key here, because when we are considering, for instance, participation rates, gender differences within older groups (in this case Veterans and Baby Boomers) exhibit more differences than for Generation X and Y. This reflects a continuing convergence in the economic and social characteristics of men and women, and when we talk of shared generational experiences between men and women it may be more valid for the younger age groups.

These differences need to be considered by employers when recruiting, training and managing their workforce. For the purpose of this report, and for ease of simplicity, we will assume that these differences are governed by generation and will therefore discuss characteristics associated with Veterans, Baby Boomers, Generation X and Generation Y as defined above, in the first instance. We will however supplement this with discussion of life stages and biological age as appropriate.

The remainder of this report will draw on the facts and figures set out in these first three chapters to examine the potential impact of generational differences on people management and make recommendations as to the HR management practices that should be adopted in order to recruit, retain and motivate a cross-generational workforce. The report will therefore be divided into different areas of HR management, namely:

- recruitment and selection
- training and development
- career development and performance management
- rewards and working patterns
- management style and leadership
- avoiding intergenerational conflict.

RECRUITMENT AND SELECTION 4

- **Employers must find ways to successfully attract employees from Generations X and Y as well as Baby Boomers into their organisations.**
- **Different generations may use different recruitment channels when looking for work – Generations X and Y may use the Internet or social networking whereas Baby Boomers may use print media or agencies.**
- **Employers need to create an employer brand that is attractive across generations.**

Recruitment is essential for the success of organisations because it provides the function of attracting human capital into the organisation and making sure that a company's workforce has the appropriate skills and abilities.

Over recent years we have seen considerable attention being paid within the national and industry media to the problems inherent in attracting Generations X and Y into the workforce. The ageing population demographics mean that these cohorts are smaller than previous ones, so there are fewer workers from Generation X and Generation Y available than there were Baby Boomers. Exacerbating this problem is the fact that Baby Boomers are now retiring, taking with them the skills and experience that many organisations rely on. This means that it is of vital importance that employers find ways to effectively attract talent from Generations X and Y to make sure that their organisation remains competitive and successful. However, recruitment does not mean only recruiting from Generations X and Y because employers may need to target jobseekers with the skills and experience possessed primarily by Baby Boomers (Crumpacker and Crumpacker 2007). Employers therefore need to find a way to attract jobseekers from across the generational spectrum. As suggested previously, the role of diversity in the recruitment process is often seen as simply spreading the net wider. Employers therefore need to consider whether they are inadvertently 'locking out' applicants from certain generations.

There are two considerations when thinking about how best to attract jobseekers from the different generations. The first is to identify recruitment channels that have the best ability to reach the generations being targeted. The second is to create an employer brand or to publicise benefits that will appeal to each generation. By combining these two factors, employers can effectively attract the talent they need into their organisation.

RECRUITMENT CHANNELS

People of different generations have different habits in the ways that they look for work and the media that they use to locate job vacancies. Baby Boomers will historically have searched for jobs by looking at advertisements in print media such as national and local newspapers and industry press, but may now use the Internet. They might also use employment agencies. The more technologically savvy Generations X and Y, however, are more likely to use electronic media, such as jobs boards and search engines like Google, so should be reached via the Internet.

Employers that are trying to recruit employees from Generations X and Y should therefore use television, Internet job sites, links to an organisation's recruitment site from a website frequently used by these groups, and websites that are popular with these generations. Generation Y in particular may also be reached via social networking websites (for some useful insights into the use of social networking websites for people management see **www.cipd.co.uk/research**).

Employers should consider marketing through search engines such as Google. Additionally, posting in concert announcements, on bulletin boards in coffee houses and certain cafes, and on flyers distributed to certain clothing stores would target recruitment efforts to the lifestyle of these generations. Employers could also advertise in daycare and child activity centres. Baby Boomers may be more effectively reached through advertising at retirement or investment seminars, on local radio segments and at health clubs and spas (Jurkiewicz 2000; Charrier 2000). They may also be reached through more traditional advertising in print media and through employment agencies. It can be seen, therefore, that a mixture of recruitment channels is needed to reach prospective employees across all four generations.

EMPLOYER BRANDING

To recruit Generations X and Y particularly employers need to market their business as a brand. These generations are made up of savvy consumers who, in consumer purchasing behaviour, are not brand loyal but are brand sensitive – they understand the promise of a particular brand (Ruch 2000). Employers must therefore apply brand management and marketing thinking to the employment experience. This can be achieved by setting up formal partnerships with the marketing team so that their marketing skills can be used for recruitment. For instance, within Orange, the telecommunications company, they have created the role of 'employer brand manager' with responsibility for issues such as recruitment marketing. This role sits between the marketing and recruitment functions of the organisation so can draw on the expertise of both. For more information on employer branding see **www.cipd.co.uk/research/_empbranding.htm**

It must be recognised that Baby Boomers and Generations X and Y will look for different things from an organisation. Therefore, an employer needs to create a 'value proposition' that will appeal to the different generations. Smith (2008) has suggested that in fact employees from all four generations want the same things, but that priorities, expectations and behaviours may differ noticeably. Smith suggests that all employees want the '3 Rs and 2 Cs'. They want to be respected, recognised and remembered, as well as to be coached and consulted. People may want the same things but want them delivered in different packages, according to when and how they grew up.

For instance, Generation X is looking for self-building opportunities, so they want an organisation that will provide the opportunity to:

- learn marketable skills (and an increasing focus on formal accreditation of skills)
- build relationships with people that can help them
- tackle challenges and produce results that will act as evidence of their ability
- manage as much of their own time as possible
- work in an entrepreneurial environment
- be creative and innovative
- work as part of a team
- receive feedback and credit for valuable contributions (Tulgan 1997).

Similarly, Generation Y is interested in organisations that:

- invest heavily in the training and development of their employees
- care about their employees as individuals
- provide clear opportunities for long-term career progression
- provide variety in daily work
- have a dynamic, forward-looking approach to the business (Terjesen, Vinnicombe and Freeman 2007).

Much less research has been done about the organisational characteristics that Baby Boomers look for when jobseeking, but we do know that, as that cohort is reaching retirement age, they might be focusing on pensions and financial security. We can also suggest that, given the characteristics of this cohort, they will be looking for organisations that provide recognition of achievement and promotion possibilities as well as the opportunity to pass on their experience through mentoring others.

Their experiences may have also made them more open to a flexible retirement or flexibility in retirement.

The research by the CIPD and Penna identified the 'value propositions' that were preferred by employees from each of the four generations.

Veterans

Veterans seek jobs that involve having authority to make decisions. They are used to clarity with regard to their roles, responsibilities and hierarchies. Veterans want to be of service to their customers. They want to feel personally valued by those around them. They expect organisations and people to reciprocate their loyalty and recognise their experience. They tend to be more engaged if people take note of their opinions and ideas. They seek personal development opportunities around coaching and development and project management.

Baby Boomers

Baby Boomers seek authority to make decisions. If they have challenging work, they are more likely to feel engaged with their organisation. Baby Boomers want work–life balance. Half would consider working beyond their expected retirement age. They want to feel personally valued by those around them and are slightly more engaged if their organisation demonstrates social/environmental responsibility. Access to personal development engages them if they feel able to be successful and there are excellent job opportunities available. They seek development opportunities around knowledge of other parts of the organisation, leadership skills, coaching and mentoring and customer service skills.

Generation X

Generation X seeks authority to make decisions and thrives on feeling challenged. They want work–life balance that gives them freedom and flexibility and have reacted against the 'face time' culture. They want to be personally valued by those around them and feel more engaged if there is a sense of team. They value feeling able to be successful in their organisation and desire access to personal development opportunities that include on-the-job growth combined with excellent development job opportunities within their organisation. They seek development that focuses on knowledge around other parts of the organisation, leadership skills, customer service skills and help with career management.

Generation Y

Generation Y seeks to be part of a team, have fun and make new friends. They feel engaged to perform better when they can access this teamworking. They also feel more engaged if they have challenging work and feel able to get things done. They want work–life balance and are more engaged with their employer if their overall benefits package meets their needs. They are also more engaged if they have access to personal development, are able to be successful and have ample opportunity to grow. These opportunities include specialist skills development. Generation Y seeks more knowledge around other parts of the organisation, leadership skills, customer service skills and project management skills.

The important lesson here is for recruiters to consider the needs of each of the groups that they are targeting and the recruitment channels that these groups will potentially use, so that they can create both a recruitment system that can reach each group but also an employer brand that is attractive across generations.

Included in the research by the CIPD and Penna is a good example of an organisation that has developed an employer brand that appeals to all but is particularly attractive to Generations X and Y – Google.

Background

Google has experienced exponential growth since it was founded ten years ago. Its technology is cutting-edge and it needs the brightest talent to continue generating great ideas and great technology. By accident, rather than design, the types of people they have employed have been young, tech-savvy and often straight from university. This is because they have the skills and ideas needed – but their objective is to recruit clever, innovative people who will fit the Google culture, regardless of their background and level of experience. The Google culture is slightly anarchic, informal, relaxed and friendly. People are not spoon fed – they are expected to stand on their own two feet and use their initiative. With their phenomenal growth and increasing competition, they have an ongoing need for new talent. They aim to present the Google 'brand' to people they want to employ now and also those who may join them in five years' time. The impression they make at any touch point in the hiring process is very important, as are word of mouth and reputation as a good employer.

Approach

- Created a 'house style' look and feel for offices – the Google primary colours, lava lamps, massive Google current search and Google Earth screens in receptions, chill-out areas – which encourages a relaxed (although highly focused) working environment.
- Every employee can have three free, high-quality meals a day in a lively canteen, plus open access to lots of areas with free drinks and snacks. This leads to informal social and business interaction and, hopefully, healthy employees.
- Culture club – lots of special interest groups to engage a broad range of interests, both professional and social.
- There is absolute consistency across all global locations in terms of technology and an office pass that can be used anywhere – so wherever people go they can plug in their laptop and work.
- The recruitment process is personal and consistent globally. After a telephone interview there are a number of one-to-ones with different people. The process suits all ages – but is potentially more favourable to experienced people. However, new graduates need to be able to deal with it. The objective is to ensure not just skills match but culture fit.

Outcomes

- still attracting some of the most talented people
- excellent retention rates
- number-one employer that graduates want to work for

TRAINING AND DEVELOPMENT 5

- **Older workers are less likely to participate in training than younger employees, possibly because of the negative attitudes of managers to training older employees, but also through choice.**
- **Generations X and Y are said to place greater emphasis on development and to want to work in an environment that supports continuous learning.**
- **The different generations may have different learning styles and prefer different modes of learning. For instance, Generations X and Y are said to prefer self-directed independent learning, using the Internet or computer-based training (CBT), whereas Baby Boomers and Veterans prefer a more traditional classroom-based learning environment.**

Moving on to consider generational or age diversity in training and development, a recent study commissioned by the Department of Innovation, Universities and Skills (Urwin et al 2009, forthcoming), has underlined the findings from previous studies that suggest that older workers are one of the groups least likely to be trained by employers (CIPD 2003). A commonly cited reason for this observation within the literature (Redman and Snape 2002; Taylor and Walker 2003) is the negative attitudes of managers towards older workers when training is considered. However, empirical studies suggest that, while older workers are less likely to be offered vocational training, there is also evidence that they are less likely to take up the opportunity when training is offered (Taylor and Urwin 2001).

Table 4 identifies a clear pattern of falling proportions of employees undertaking employer-provided training as we move upwards through the age distribution and this is particularly pronounced for men. Thus, the proportion of male employees aged between 16 and 24 who undertook employer-provided training in the previous three months was 31.5%, compared with only 17.9% for the 50–59/64 age group. For women the difference is not as pronounced, with a gap of only 8.2% separating the corresponding proportions (34.3% and 26.1%). However, considering those who have not undergone job-related education and training in the past three months, it would seem that much of the differences between men and women (as well as older and younger cohorts) are being driven by differential rates of take-up at different ages. When one considers the proportions that had either experienced *or* been offered training, any differences by age are much reduced for men and reversed for women.

Table 4: Proportion of males and females in employment undergoing or offered job-related education or training in the last three months, by age (%)

Male	16–24	25–39	40–49	50–64	65–75	All ages
undertook job-related training in last three months	31.5	24.5	24.0	17.9	8.4	23.2
did not undertake job-related training in last three months	68.5	75.5	76.0	82.1	91.6	76.8
offered training, but **did not** undertake job-related training in last three months	46.1	59.3	59.2	65.3	66.3	59.0
undertook or offered job-related training in last three months	58.5	60.1	58.9	51.6	24.9	56.7
Total frequency	1,967,268	5,398,750	3,872,757	3,865,113	355,437	15,459,325
Female	**16–24**	**25–39**	**40–49**	**50–64**	**65–75**	**All ages**
undertook job-related training in last three months	34.3	31.3	31.3	26.1	12.4	30.2
did not undertake job-related training in last three months	65.7	68.7	68.7	73.9	87.6	69.8
offered training, but **did not** undertake job-related training in last three months	44.9	55.0	55.7	59.7	64.9	55.1
undertook or offered job-related training in last three months	62.2	69.6	70.5	64.8	35.2	67.1
Total frequency	1,767,460	4,452,598	3,442,814	3,182,155	197,176	13,042,203

Source: *Labour Force Survey* (2007)

There are many possible reasons for the lower incidence of training in later years. According to human capital theory, firms and individuals undertake investment in their human capital if the net present value of future incremental earnings accruing from the investment outweigh the direct and opportunity costs. Thus, we may expect age to have a significant effect on the viability of any such investment. The length of the future income stream accruing to an older worker is likely to be shorter than that for a younger worker. This may be expected to reduce the incentive for investment in human capital, from both the individual and firm perspective – though it should be noted that older workers have lower levels of turnover than their younger counterparts and this may be expected to offset some of the reduction in incentives from the organisation's viewpoint.

Most of the attention in research and in the literature has focused on effective ways of training and developing Generation X. Generation X is characterised as placing great emphasis on development and generally liking to work in an environment that supports continuous learning. Generation X employees want stimulating jobs so they can continue learning and will be more likely to stay with an organisation that allows them this (Corley 1999). Generation X particularly values mentoring relationships in the workplace where mentors and organisational leaders must lead by example. Mentors should be flexible, embody the values they profess, be nurturing, give frequent feedback and appreciate the diversity of the generation.

Individuals from Generation X are said to have developed a shorter attention span, so it is suggested that more formal training materials need to take this into account. For example, videos shouldn't be more than 15 minutes long (Filipczak 1994). However, in contrast, it has been suggested that they do have the ability to concentrate on multiple tasks at the same time. In addition, Generation X and Y's way of learning was shaped by computer technology, so they like innovation and have an ability to assimilate seemingly unrelated pieces of information. Generation X prefers to learn using multiple sources (Tulgan 1996). Generation X wants to know why they should learn something before they will take the time to learn how.

Given this, the implication is that training should focus on outcomes rather than techniques and on what they will be able to do rather than what they will know. Training experiences should be meaningful, memorable and fun, as Generation X is used to being entertained. To do this organisations should try to use all six senses and should allow time for trainees to practise. Individuals from Generation X like self-study so employers should put training material on video and audiotapes, interactive CDs and in self-paced manuals and workbooks so that they are responsible for their own learning. Generation X doesn't like inflexibility, being overmanaged or overwatched, disparaging comments, feeling disrespected, focusing on techniques or hearing about past experiences, so trainers should focus on end results, be flexible, emphasise visuals and provide continuous education (Caudron 1997).

The recent *Who Learns at Work?* survey from the CIPD (2008d) found that employees' favoured method of learning is not being matched to the type of training that they receive. This research showed that being shown how to do things and practising them was overwhelmingly considered the best method of learning, with 46% of respondents citing this as preferred. The research also showed that 50% of younger employees (Generation Y) preferred this method, therefore questioning the assumption described above that this group's learning preferences are different from older employees.

To encourage learning in Generation X, employers should (Bova and Kroth 2001):

- Use action learning with the emphasis on reflection and structured so that real issues are solved.
- Encourage incidental learning both through action learning and in the workplace. This is unstructured and dependent on circumstance.
- Promote a culture of forgiveness, open-mindedness and awareness.
- Use formal learning with opportunities for self-direction, such as e-learning emphasised over structured classroom training.
- Use a human touch in development, such as mentors and leaders. These individuals should lead by example.
- Adopt special programmes such as job rotations, stretch assignments, taskforce leadership, mentoring and new product development assignments so that employees take on more responsibility while being supported by more experienced people.

In contrast, Baby Boomers prefer personal interaction, so traditional classroom-based training should be used to a greater degree with this group. While Baby Boomers may not like to be taught with technology as much, they do like to keep up with emerging technology and like the opportunity to continue improving their skills and knowledge, so should be provided with the training to do this (McCafferty 2003).

Veterans prefer a more formal approach to training so are most comfortable when training consists of lectures, seminars or presentations from topic experts. They like information that is well researched, organised and supported by facts, figures and examples. They will prefer a book, tape or article to resources online or computer-based training (Berl 2006).

Generation Y also place great emphasis on training. Research from the Chartered Institute of Management (Macleod 2008) found that the vast majority (97%) of young managers were looking to build their transferable skills. Generation Y managers were greatly self-directed when it came to their learning and personal development, with 68% initiating most of their learning themselves. The literature has suggested that to develop Generation Y, employers should steer away from articles and books in training and encourage them to access resources online or direct them to computer-based training. Content in presentations should be kept brief with bullet points, lists and graphics. The organisation should be promoted as a learning organisation so that Generation Y will gain knowledge, skills and responsibility. They should also be helped to inventory, understand and value what they are learning each day and helped to realise that training is an important part of their duties for addressing real-time job responsibilities and professional development (Berl 2006).

Recent research from the CIPD and London Business School (CIPD 2008c) provided a number of examples of organisations using innovative approaches to training to address the needs of Generation Y. For instance, Bytes Technology Group provided tailored, bite-sized training modules for employees.

Finally, there is evidence that computer usage rises between the ages of 20 and 45 and declines after the age of 50 (Card and DiNardo 2002), for the present working population. In contrast, ICT is increasingly popular as a method to assist learning, predominantly in the form of e-learning tools such as: learning portals, training guides, games, simulations and virtual classrooms (Schank 2005). The pedagogical value of online learning approaches has been widely reported (for example Richards 2003, Salmon 2004) and it is usually perceived that the interactive approach to learning, supported by e-learning technologies, is an ideal medium for individual learning, cognitive support and reflective thinking.

There is a clear need to question the view that e-learning technologies (for detailed information about e-learning see the CIPD resources available at **www.cipd.co.uk**) are an ideal support medium for all; it is quite possible that there is something intrinsic to ICT that may present barriers to the over-50s. In contrast, this may be a purely generational effect, as it is hard to see the ageing Generation Y developing an aversion to ICT.

The research by the CIPD and Penna includes a useful case study – McDonald's – that illustrates the use of career development to meet generational needs.

Business case

The Generation Y cohort makes up almost 75% of the McDonald's workforce. Training and development is recognised as a key career anchor for Generation Y and one that, if organisations get it right for this generation, will seek to attract, engage and retain them. Therefore, training and development not only plays a fundamental part in helping McDonald's to effectively attract, engage and retain such a large proportion of its workforce but is also critical in maintaining high levels of customer service and quality. With such a large percentage of employees from one particular generation, McDonald's has developed a bespoke training and development offering, accommodating the needs, expectations and behaviours of Generation Y, rather than placing the majority of its workforce into a predefined training and development plan.

Approach

Key to the success of this approach was the recognition and acceptance that Generation Y employees were different. The training and development had to be adapted to keep them engaged and maximise their performance. When McDonald's explored exactly what this difference looked like, they found Generation Y to be superb multitaskers, with the ability to quickly absorb information from myriad channels that frequently offer information centred on audio-visual stimulation.

Generation Y has built up an incredibly strong sense of loyalty to friends and peer groups. McDonald's therefore found that within a training environment, the preference of Generation Y is to work collaboratively. They also demand immediate feedback. McDonald's have therefore redesigned their training programmes taking these distinct behaviours into account, ensuring that programmes use the latest technology to provide training that facilitates multitasking that is filled with audio-visual information, allows a collaborative approach and provides opportunities for instant feedback.

Outcomes

A study showed that 90% of McDonald's staff showed high levels of employee engagement. The key contributing factors in this high level of engagement among McDonald's employees were the opportunities for training and development offered by the organisation.

CAREER DEVELOPMENT AND PERFORMANCE MANAGEMENT

6

- **Different generations are said to have different attitudes towards careers – Veterans and Baby Boomers tend to believe that a job is for life whereas Generations X and Y change jobs regularly.**
- **Older employees may find their careers 'plateaued' and may generally find it more difficult to change careers or organisations.**
- **Generations X and Y define career success as work–life balance and developing marketable skills, whereas Baby Boomers focus more on promotion and recognition within an organisation.**
- **Generations X and Y require frequent and immediate feedback.**

The proposed differences between generations, particularly Generation X and Baby Boomers, are perceived to be most pronounced in relation to their attitudes towards careers. This is an area that has been the subject of much discussion in both academia and in practice.

Baby Boomers were brought up to believe that a job was for life and therefore generally will have had a maximum of around four jobs within their lifetime. Traditionally, Baby Boomers tend to stay with one organisation for a long time, perhaps even their entire career. Their unwritten employment contract states that if they work hard, are loyal and do as they are told they will be rewarded with secure jobs, steady pay increases and financial security (Ansoorian, Good and Samuelson 2003).

Unlike Generation Xers, who assume responsibility for their own career development in a boundaryless career environment where sideways or even downwards moves may be common (Arthur and Rousseau 1996), Baby Boomers continue to regard a 'career' as a linear series of upward moves, largely employer-controlled. But reality has partly mitigated this view: this generation witnessed or was involved in the redundancies of the 1980s and early 1990s and thereafter has directly experienced the fallout resulting from increasing globalisation of employing organisations and the flattening of internal hierarchical organisational systems (Sullivan, Carden and Martin 1998). At its most fundamental level this new employment context has 'destroyed the implicit labour contract linking seniority with security' (Moen 2005, p189).

Despite the recent introduction of age discrimination legislation in the UK, Veterans and Baby Boomers are aware that they are the generations most likely to be culled in an economic downturn. Certainly they are aware that they will find it more difficult than earlier in their careers to change jobs or obtain new employment if made redundant (Daniel and Heywood 2007) due to the continuing barriers maintained by inherent ageist attitudes in the workplace (Loretto and White 2006).

In terms of Baby Boomers' career development, many of the factors that may be thought of as age-related are in fact more likely to be related to tenure. For example, by the time they reach their late forties or fifties, those who have been with an organisation for some years are likely to find themselves stalled or plateaued and facing a situation of no further upward promotions or pay increases (Ettington 1997). This may present difficulties in terms of motivating older employees, who may be facing limited new challenges and a declining sense of value. The situation frequently also creates an organisational 'log jam', effectively preventing the further upward promotion of Generation Xers. This situation is likely to worsen as Baby Boomers continue to work longer.

A number of factors, such as relationships, pension arrangements, management and leadership responsibilities, act to increase what has been termed the 'occupational embeddedness' of older workers, encouraging them to remain in situ even where external opportunities for career progression exist (Ng and Feldman 2007). On the other hand, those Baby Boomers with good financial provision and possibly well-developed plans for the future (for example retiring abroad, starting up a business) may welcome early retirement packages.

Workers from Generation X, on the other hand, having seen their parents' loyalty to their employer rewarded in the 1980s with losing their jobs through redundancy, tend to change jobs regularly and frequently based on the available opportunities and rewards. Generation X tends to hop from job to job and have 'one eye in the company and one eye outside all the time' (Filipczak 1994). They expect promotions or at least lateral moves frequently because they get bored quickly and will want to move on, either within the same company or to another. Because Generation X workers have not experienced job security, they see jobs as stepping stones to something else. They may therefore leave a job seeking greater satisfaction elsewhere (McCafferty 2003). Individuals from Generation X are seen as loyal only to themselves and their personal goals; they will develop skills and apply them effectively, for which they expect their employer to listen to their needs, create an enabling environment and pay them fairly. Generation X can be 'corporate nomads' (Ansoorian, Good and Samuelson 2003), using employers for skill-building purposes and changing employers without the slightest reservations.

The careers literature on Generation Y suggests a growing development of micro-careers, where tenure in any one job is relatively short and young managers are more willing to change job frequently. However, research from the Chartered Institute of Management (Macleod 2008) found that, while there was a trend towards shorter stays with any one organisation for a third of young managers, there was still a significant proportion of young managers who stayed with organisations on a longer-term basis. Thirty-one per cent had been in their current jobs for more than six years, and 32% had been in their job for between three and five years.

The definition of career success in both Generations X and Y have been shown to be focused on achieving balance in work and life, individualising success and shaping one's own definition of success from a range of factors (McDonald and Hite 2008). This has implications for human resource development (HRD) in that, in managing employees from Generations X and Y, employers will need to move away from the traditional view of career development as advancement and adopt a more broad-based view that acknowledges subjective, as well as objective, goals and the likelihood that employees will not be with the organisation for all of their careers. Generations X and Y value informal learning opportunities such as seeking out challenging opportunities and taking the initiative on new projects. They also value networking and work–life balance. They may respond well to peer groups or mentoring. This also means that HRD needs to find new ways of evaluating career development in ways that are not based on advancement. This may include career satisfaction, work–life balance and employability. Therefore the steps needed to manage the career of an employee from Generation X and Y might be very different from those needed to manage the careers of Baby Boomers, who respond better to more traditional methods of career development and to formal career advancement schemes linked to pay.

Even within a generation the existence of a single homogeneous group with common aspirations cannot be assumed. For example, numerous studies have shown that women's career needs and drivers are quite different from those of men, with women tending to rate success in terms of internal criteria, while men continue to pursue position, pay and status (Sturges 1999; Powell and Mainiero 1992; Roberts and Friend 1998). Particularly within the Veteran and Baby Boomer generations, women's career development may have encompassed broken career paths and be facing continuing challenges caused by caring responsibilities.

PERFORMANCE MANAGEMENT

The generations also require different treatment in performance management. When addressing performance concerns with Veterans, employers should describe the problem and how it affects the team or organisation goals and solicit their ideas before suggesting ways in which they can improve their performance. For Baby Boomers, peer feedback should be used to improve performance. It is also important to recognise and reward their work ethic, dedication and long hours (Berl 2006). Employees from Generation X, on the other hand, require frequent and immediate feedback with credit for good performance.

Demographic, social and economic changes are now seeing many Baby Boomers and Veterans either having to, or wanting to, work longer (McNair, Flynn and Owen 2004) and this, combined with the increasing abolition of mandatory retirement ages following the 2006 age discrimination legislation, means that employers must increasingly performance-manage older workers to avoid an open-ended and potentially problematic situation. But performance management of older workers may mask prejudice and be based on erroneous assumptions (Ferris and King 1992); older employees may receive more severe penalties (for example transfer or demotion) as a consequence of poor performance than younger colleagues, who receive recommendations for training (Rupp, Vodanovich and Credé 2005). Added to this can be the reluctance of younger managers to effectively address performance issues in older individuals (Finkelstein and Burke 1998).

REWARDS AND WORKING PATTERNS 7

- **Money motivates all four generations but employees of different ages may value other financial and non-financial rewards differently.**
- **Generations X and Y are said to place particular emphasis on flexible working. However, the desire to work flexibly has also been shown to increase as employees approach retirement age.**
- **Retirement and pension provision is of particular importance to Baby Boomers because of their particular life stage.**

It has been suggested that the different generations place different degrees of value on different rewards.

Money is an important motivator of all four generations. Baby Boomers value recognition in the form of salary increases, while Generation X has grown up during depressed economic circumstances so value money for its own sake. A Chartered Management Institute report (Macleod 2008) notes that Generation Y face considerable financial pressures as the first generation to pay for higher education tuition fees, but may now suffer less from house price inflation. The report suggested that 41% of Generation Y managers lived in rented accommodation or with parents and 39% earned less than £25,000. Indeed, recent research from *Personnel Today Magazine* (Berry 2008) showed that over half of Generation Y employees (68%) said that salary and benefits were very important. Recognition for good work (54%) and holiday entitlement (47%) were also seen as important to Generation Y employees (Berry 2008).

Employees of different ages will, however, value other financial and non-financial benefits differently. For instance, it has been suggested that employees from Generation Y want competitive salaries, diversity in projects, good benefits, learning opportunities paid for by the company, travel opportunities and flexible work hours. Baby Boomers on the other hand prefer retirement planning and place particular emphasis on economic security (McCafferty 2003). Baby Boomers are generally more focused on materialistic pursuits, while Generation X is focused on peace of mind and leisure time (Carlson 2004). Generation X is also driven by non-financial rewards such as receiving personal credit for tangible results, increased responsibility, opportunities for creative expression and exposure to decision-makers. Financially, Generation X employees like incentive-based pay and stock ownership (Corley 1999).

As different generations value different rewards, it may therefore be recommended that employers should consider a cafeteria or flexible approach to benefits that allows employees to select their own benefits package within a predefined financial limit. This also helps employers avoid the expense of providing benefits that are unwanted and unused (Jurkiewicz 2000; Charrier 2000). It has been suggested that Generation X employees in particular appreciate flexible benefits to give them the opportunity of making decisions based on their individual lifestyles and needs (Corley 1999).

It is important for Generation X that rewards should be concrete and should quickly follow the behaviour being rewarded. Generation X employees like to know what is being rewarded and how it is being measured, so linking pay to clear performance management systems is important (Filipczak 1994).

RETIREMENT PROVISION

The issue of reward has received attention in the existing literature that considers the implications of generational diversity for HR practice (see, for instance, Dencker, Joshi and Martocchio 2007). There are many dimensions to this issue, but with respect to our previous discussions both age and generational factors are at work when we consider the changing nature of retirement income. As one might expect, the suggestion is that moving upwards through the age distribution the prospect of retirement looms larger and increasing proportions of individuals have some form of coverage. Research by Disney and Tanner (1999) into the results of the 1988–89 and 1994 *Retirement Surveys* suggested that expectations of retirement are often fulfilled, with just over half of their sample of respondents retiring when they expected.

Together with the two-tier state pension provision and employer occupational pension schemes, there are now a wide range of personal pension plans open to individuals; and their proliferation partly reflects the decline in occupational schemes (particularly those that offer defined benefits). The growth in personal pensions can be traced back to the 1986 Social Security Act, which allowed employees to choose whether they wished to participate in an employer's scheme, and also extended the contracting-out option to personal pensions and employer-provided defined-contribution (DC) schemes.

The move from occupational to personal pension plans mirrors a wider switch from defined benefit (often final salary) schemes to ones where there are defined contributions. This has contributed to a growing concern that individuals are not putting enough away for their retirement. For instance, the Turner Commission (2004) suggests that between 9 and 12 million people who are members of defined-contribution schemes are not providing adequately for their retirement. Initiatives designed to stimulate private pension saving are not working and individuals (employees) are shouldering an increasing burden of the risk associated with this.

WORKING PATTERNS

Much of the literature on generational diversity to date has focused on working patterns because this is seen to be where much of the ascribed differences between generations are thought to have an impact for HR. For instance, it is claimed that Generation X are more focused on work–life balance than the Baby Boomers. Of particular importance to Generation X is the balance of work and family life. Research has shown that Generation X were most likely to have childcare responsibilities, whereas Veterans may be caring for elderly relatives. Not surprisingly, then, problems with the spillover of work into home life is most common in Baby Boomers (Dilworth and Kingsbury 2005). Baby Boomers are willing to work long hours in return for recognition and financial rewards, but employees from Generation X are particularly wary of 'workaholism' and like to have flexibility in their working hours so that they can put their family before their job (Filipczak 1994). It could be said that Baby Boomers 'live to work' whereas Generation X 'works to live' (McCafferty 2003). Generation Y also has strong family values and want flexible work hours. Research from the Chartered Institute of Management suggested that working away from the workplace was also common in Generation Y managers, with 49% of the managers surveyed working away from the office at least some of the time.

The evidence for the increased focus on flexible working in Generations X and Y is, however, mixed and it is quite possible that the protracted boom between the mid-1990s and 2008 (with only a small dip in the real economy in 2000–01) has made all generations more focused on work–life balance, as they have the luxury to do so in a more favourable labour market. CIPD research on managing an ageing workforce (2008b), as discussed in Chapter 2, has shown that flexible working is also important to older workers. In fact, this research suggested that the importance of work–life balance had increased as employees neared retirement age, therefore contradicting the suggestion that flexible working is particularly important for younger workers.

An analysis of the use of flexible working arrangements by age/generation supports the idea that flexible working actually increases with age. Tables 5 and 6 draw on two existing data sources to shed light on the differences that exist across generations.

Table 5: Flexible working by generation* (%)

	Use flexible working (any)	Part-time working	Remote working	Flexitime
Generation Y	12	9	9	15
Generation X	23	21	14	15
Baby Boomers	19	11	16	11
Veterans	41	25	14	26

* Taken from research by Kelliher and Anderson (2008)

We can examine this in more detail through an analysis of data relating to part-time working. Part-time working is not the only form of flexible working, but it is one of the most widespread alternatives for those who wish to balance caring or other commitments. The importance of part-time working among female members of the workforce is well documented and Table 6 underlines this. Furthermore, for both men and women, there is a tendency for the proportion of individuals who are working part-time to increase as we move upwards through the age groups. However, as one might expect, part-time working is particularly popular among those at the extremes of the age distribution.

Table 6: Percentage of employed males and females within each age group working full-time or part-time

Males	16–24	25–39	40–49	50–64	65–75
Full-time	1,527,916 (73.3%)	5,168,433 (95.4%)	3,724,451 (95.8%)	3,417,855 (88.3%)	127,661 (35.9%)
Part-time	556,264 (27.0%)	251,412 (3.8%)	161,931 (3.9%)	453,919 (10.4%)	227,776 (63.2%)
Total frequency (males)	2,084,180	5,419,845	3,886,382	3,871,774	355,437
Females					
Full-time	1,073,263 (56.1%)	2,827,661 (63.3%)	2,007,142 (58.1%)	1,695,440 (53.2%)	35,955 (18.2%)
Part-time	840,038 (43.9%)	1,637,061 (36.7%)	1,444,974 (41.9%)	1,494,696 (46.9%)	161,655 (81.8%)
Total frequency (females)	1,913,301	4,464,722	3,452,116	3,190,136	197,610

Source: *Labour Force Survey*, Quarter 1, 2007.

Table 7 identifies the reasons for the distribution of part-time working. As can be seen, those aged 16–24 are much more likely to take a part-time job because they are still studying, while individuals who have passed retirement age simply do not want to work full-time. Furthermore, in contrast with the situation among women, where the vast majority of those aged between 25 and state pension age (SPA) are working part-time because they did not want a full-time position, almost one-third of men between 25 and 49 who are working part-time do so because they could not find a full-time job. For those men between 50 and 64 who are working part-time, there is some evidence that they have opted to work part-time to ease the transition into full retirement.

Table 7: Reasons for employed males and females working part-time within each age group (%)

Reason for part-time job (males)	16–24	25–39	40–49	50–64	65–75
Student or at school	75.7	23.1	*	*	0.0
Ill or disabled	*	6.3	9.8	8.1	*
Could not find full-time job	15.4	33.2	31.0	12.2	*
Did not want full-time job	8.2	37.4	55.1	79.3	96.6
Total frequency (males)	554,370	246,153	157,022	451,936	225,404
Reason for part-time job (females)					
Student or at school	68.5	4.4	1.2	*	0.0
Ill or disabled	*	1.5	1.9	2.9	*
Could not find full-time job	14.2	6.1	6.3	6.0	*
Did not want full-time job	16.8	88.0	90.6	90.6	97.6
Total frequency (females)	835,542	1,628,381	1,436,590	1,489,599	161,655

Source: *Labour Force Survey*, Quarter 1, 2007

*cell size unreliable because less than 10,000

The level of dissatisfaction among male temporary workers is even higher than for those men who work part-time. Similarly, between 20% and 30% of women aged between 16 and 59 who are working under temporary arrangements would have preferred a permanent position. However, it is still the case that the proportion of temporary workers who are dissatisfied with their position tends to fall as we analyse older groups of males and females when compared with younger males and females aged 25–49. When one considers the extent to which each age group is engaged in temporary working, there is a clear tendency for the youngest and oldest age groups to undertake work of this type and also to have done so out of choice.

What these tables hide is the increasing convergence in employment profiles of men and women, with the numbers of men of all age groups working part-time nearly doubling between 1993 and 2008 to 1.8 million, compared with an increase for women of around 13%. When one considers the age of Generation X at this point in time (27–47), they are the generation having children, and it may be more appropriate to consider the postponement of childbirth for many women in recent years and the associated increase in men who take on childcare responsibilities as the driver for any intergenerational differences. Thus, to understand the implications for employers one needs to look behind simplistic statements that suggest Generation X are more focused on work–life balance and consider whether this is something they will carry with them into their later years (when they constitute an older generation), or simply a reflection of their point in the life cycle.

MANAGEMENT STYLE AND LEADERSHIP 8

- **The different generations prefer to be managed in different ways. For instance, Generation X does not like authoritarian leadership but prefers informality and being trusted to act independently.**
- **Generation Y likes to have fun at work and to be allowed opportunities for socialising.**
- **Veterans and Baby Boomers like to be respected and for their experience to be acknowledged.**
- **Employers should pay particular attention to management style when an individual is being managed by someone from a different generation than their own.**

There has been some specific discussion of the issues that arise from generational diversity when one considers *management style and leadership*. However, this is the area where most care needs to be taken over the claims made, as we have less empirical and/or theoretical evidence to draw on. The proposition is that different values and characteristics of Veterans, Baby Boomers, Generation X and Generation Y mean that they respond differently to different management or leadership styles. If this is the case, then it is important that employers realise this and alter their management techniques accordingly if they are to effectively retain and motivate employees from across generations.

The work factors that are favoured by Veterans (Matures), Baby Boomers and Generation X (GenXers) have been summarised by Jurkiewicz and Brown (1998) in Table 8.

Table 8: Work factors favoured by each generation

GenXers	Chance to learn new things, chance to engage in satisfying leisure activities, chance to exercise leadership, chance to use their special abilities, chance to make a contribution to important decisions, freedom from supervision, freedom from pressures to conform both on and off the job, opportunity for advancement and variety in job assignments.
Boomers	A stable and secure future, chance to benefit society, high salary, high prestige and social status, and freedom from pressures to conform both on and off the job.
Matures	A stable and secure future, friendly and congenial associates and working as part of a team.

There has been considerable discussion of the implications of these preferences on the management of different generations, again particularly in reference to Generation X.

It is generally agreed that Generation X doesn't really want to be managed. Generation X employees do want managers to take responsibility for things but not to be authoritarian. Individuals from Generation X don't buy into the concept of 'line of sight managing' but like informality and have a more casual approach to authority, therefore formal hierarchies may be lost on them. Managers should treat them as individuals rather than as groups and avoid micromanaging them.

Managers must learn to know when it is best to intervene and provide answers and when to back off, letting them work it out for themselves.

Managers have to be more like parents to be effective, to be personally involved in the lives of the people they manage and to give employees individual attention and constant feedback. This requires good interpersonal skills and managers' time (Filipczak 1994).

Managers should adopt a management style that demonstrates the value of their expertise and invite subordinates to participate in decision-making. They want to know that they are part of decision-making and feel that they are contributing to something bigger than themselves. They also want to know that significant operating decisions are tied to a clear direction and set of operating values (Hessen and Lewis 2001). Generation X is not impressed by authority or a management structure that does not encourage participation or teamwork.

To motivate Generation X employees, managers need to reward innovation, make public displays of success, support personal growth, create opportunities for satisfying teamwork and personal responsibility, help subordinates achieve visibility in the organisation and create a culture of fun. To retain employees from this generation, employers need to offer variety, stimulation and constant change to maintain their interest, trust them to get the job done and give them the freedom and flexibility to set their own hours (Tulgan 1996).

Losyk (1997) summarised the principles of managing Generation X:

- Accept them and learn to work with them rather than fight them.
- Use love and caring because they need to know that you truly care about them as people.
- Support them outside work and show support for them through difficult personal situations.
- Don't baby them – they want to be seen as independent and self-starters while being guided and cared for.
- Be hands off but be there, give them freedom and independence and don't micromanage them.
- Ask, ask, ask – ask lots of questions and implement solutions.
- Discuss your methods and explain how you like to manage and evaluate them.
- Train and orient them by meeting with them often because training is a key motivator; develop mentoring programmes.
- Set specific standards.
- Make work fun.

Generation Y is focused on having fun at work, therefore those managing this cohort should emphasise the fun side of the workplace and provide a variety of activities that the employee can enjoy. Generation Y should be provided with opportunities for socialising and building networks with colleagues. The best way to communicate with Generation Y is through the use of technology, by using company blogs and websites.

Managers can establish rapport with Veterans by acknowledging their background and experience and seeking to understand what is motivating them. Managers should gain agreement from Veterans before formulating action plans and avoid situations where these individuals might lose face with younger colleagues (Berl 2006).

When managing Baby Boomers, managers should let them know that they are respected and make their accomplishments known. Managers should get to know Boomer employees personally, value their experience in the organisation and appeal to their desire to make a difference by presenting challenges as opportunities to solve problems. Managers should also encourage their participation in decision-making (Berl 2006). Boomers prefer to use face-to-face communication rather than to communicate electronically.

Particular difficulties may arise within organisations where employees report to a manager from a younger generation than their own. Research from the Society for Human Resource Management (Burke 2004) showed that 90% of the US organisations surveyed contained employees who reported to a manager or supervisor younger than themselves. In this scenario, it is particularly important that generational differences in values and preferences for management style are considered. It should be noted, however, that the same research found that the majority of respondents who had employees reporting to a younger manager or supervisor (70%) were not aware of any complaints stemming from this. Among those that had received complaints, the most common was that the subordinate from an older generation felt that the younger manager may have qualifications but did not have sufficient real-world knowledge and experience. Other reasons for complaint were problems with the supervisor's management style, the subordinate not respecting the supervisor due to their age and the employees' failure to understand each other's problems and concerns. These issues may be overcome through management development and training, team-building and mediation.

It should also be noted that many managers might have stereotypical impressions of older or younger workers. Research from Cranfield School of Management (2007) found that age-related stereotypes were prevalent among HR managers – older workers were seen as resistant to change, uninterested in training and new technology, and slow to learn, whereas younger workers were seen as more likely to take time off sick and less likely to stay in the job. Negative attitudes of this kind may add to any conflict between generations in the workplace.

AVOIDING GENERATIONAL OR AGE 'CONFLICT' 9

- **The differences between generations or 'generation gap' may lead to conflict within the workplace.**
- **Baby Boomers and Generation X view the concept of work differently – Baby Boomers may view Generation X as disrespectful slackers while Generation X sees Baby Boomers as overcautious and worshipping hierarchy.**
- **Employers should play to the values and experience of each generation and emphasise the importance of communication.**
- **Age can also lead to conflict within the workplace because older employees are often viewed less favourably by employers.**

Differences in the attitudes and behaviours displayed by generations are often described as a 'generation gap'. At work the distinctions between generations is becoming increasingly complex as multi-generation gaps emerge. The existence of up to four different generations – Veterans, Baby Boomers, Generation X and Generation Y – within the workforce may be the cause of a certain degree of conflict in the workplace.

In particular, it has been suggested that the stark differences in values between the Baby Boomers and Generation X means that they are on a 'collision course' (Karp and Sirias 2001). Generation X is seen as differing from Baby Boomers in such significant ways that, if not addressed, may have a negative effect on co-operative working relationships (Ansoorian, Good and Samuelson 2003).

US survey research from the Society of Human Resource Management (Burke 2004) found that 40% of HR professionals were aware of intergenerational conflict within their workplace (see Figure 3). This research showed that workers from large organisations were much more likely to

Figure 3 ✣ Awareness of intergenerational conflict

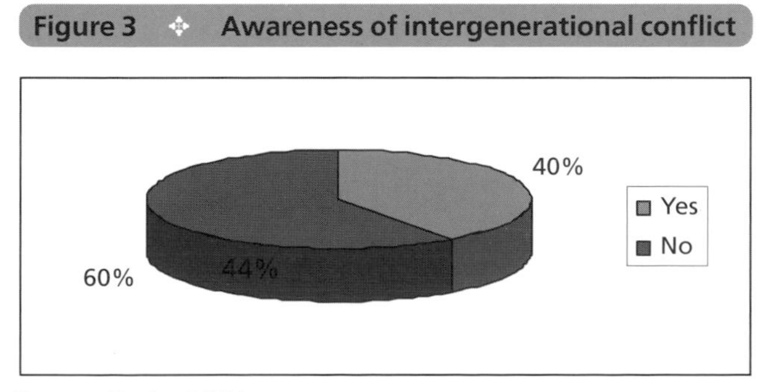

Source: Burke 2004

report intergenerational conflict than those from small or medium-sized organisations (58% compared with 31% and 34% respectively). It is possible that these percentages may in reality be even higher as, in some instances, intergenerational conflict may not escalate to the point where HR professionals become aware of it.

What sort of evidence has been presented on this issue? A main factor in the conflict between Generation X and Baby Boomers is their divergent belief systems, which can lead to misunderstanding and 'finger pointing' because the two generations view the concept of work differently. Service-oriented, driven, team-player Baby Boomers are seen by Generation X as being self-righteous, workaholic, political animals. In turn, Baby Boomers see Generation X's adaptable, techno-literate independents as slackers who lack social skills and spend too much time on the Internet. Both Baby Boomers and Veterans might view Generation X as being disrespectful of rules and authority, lacking employer loyalty and scornful of paying dues to move up the ladder. Generation X sees Baby Boomers as overcautious, hierarchy-worshipping and overly influenced by their parents' 'depression mentality'. In addition, Generation X employees might feel misunderstood and mismanaged.

This situation is worsened by the fact that generally department heads within organisations are often Baby Boomers, more junior members of staff are from Generation X, while Generation Y is entering the workforce. This can cause difficulties. Conflict between the two groups is evident because Baby Boomers aren't retiring and therefore aren't making room for Generation X up the hierarchical ladder. One obstacle to bridging the generation gap is the lack of acceptance of Generation X by Baby Boomers. Baby Boomers often focus on issues pertinent to them, such as retirement, rather than those that are important to Generation X employees. Baby Boomers might have difficulty adjusting to the influx of Generation X into the workforce because they have a different approach to work (O'Bannon 2001). Boomers often believe (and resent) the fact that Generation X and Y do not work as long or hard as they do. This might be because they work from remote locations, telecommute or have a virtual office so are not visible. Generations X and Y are results-oriented and do not care how or where they work, plus they also feel that they need to balance work and home (Glass 2007).

These differences can be reconciled by playing to the values and beliefs of each group. Managers should let Baby Boomers know that their experience is valued while showing Generations X and Y that the organisation is a fun place to work. Successful leaders will continue to differentiate their treatment, providing Baby Boomers with recognition and opportunities for input while giving Generation X the simultaneous tasks and projects, and frequent, timely and specific feedback that it desires. However, this differentiation can lead to resentment and conflict when Baby Boomers feel that Generation X is moving in on its turf too quickly and Generation X thinks Baby Boomers are too entrenched in their positions.

The key to overcoming this is communication. However, communication methods can also cause problems because Baby Boomers value face-to-face communication and will get up and go to someone else's office to speak to them, whereas Generation X will use whatever method is more convenient and Generation Y prefers to use instant messaging, text and email. Expectation of feedback can also cause problems because Baby Boomers work with very little feedback, whereas Generations X and Y like and expect constant feedback. This can cause conflict when a Generation X employee manages a Baby Boomer because the Baby Boomer may feel insulted by specific instructions, whereas the younger worker feels lost without specific guidance. The ability to work with people who span age groups is becoming a critical management skill. Baby Boomer managers need to understand what drives Generation X employees to coach them successfully and to grow and retain them.

Any consideration of generational conflict or a generation gap needs to take into account the evidence on views towards age. As Urwin (2004) suggests, there is a surprising degree of commonality of views towards ageing and retirement across the generations. First, Table 9 sets out the views of individuals on the extent to which they consider employers in Britain to view older job applicants less favourably. While the proportion that consider that employers discriminate against older individuals 'a lot' increases as we move upwards through the age distribution, it is interesting to note that the perception of discrimination against this group is still strong among the young, though they are more likely than older individuals to consider that it happens 'sometimes'.

Table 9: Responses to the question: 'how often do you think that employers in Britain refuse a job to an applicant only because he or she is aged over 50?' (%)

	18–24	25–39	40–49	50–59/64	60/65–75	All ages
A lot	45.5	49.3	61.5	67.8	67.7	58.8
Sometimes	46.8	43.5	35.2	28.1	25.3	35.5
Hardly ever	3.8	2.4	0.6	1.9	1.4	1.9
Can't choose	3.2	4.1	2.5	1.5	4.9	3.2
Not answered	0.6	0.7	0.3	0.7	0.7	0.6
Total frequency	156	542	358	413	288	1,757

Source: British Social Attitudes Survey (2000)

Table 10 sets out people's views towards these perceived discriminatory practices, with individuals of all ages (59%) likely to consider this as something that is usually or always wrong – though one-quarter of those aged between 18 and 24 do seem ambivalent. Despite this, there are encouraging signs and, given that some time has now elapsed since these data were collected, one may hope for an even more favourable picture as the introduction of age discrimination legislation will have served to further raise awareness of these issues.

Table 10: Responses to the question: 'do you think it's right to refuse a job applicant simply because they are aged over 50?' (%)

	18–24	25–39	40–49	50–59/64	60/65–75	All ages
Always right	1.3	0.2	0.6	0.7	1.4	0.7
Usually right	3.8	3.1	3.1	2.9	1.4	2.8
Neither right nor wrong	25.0	13.1	9.2	9.5	11.5	12.2
Usually wrong	43.6	48.9	48.3	50.5	47.2	48.4
Always wrong	21.8	28.6	35.5	34.5	33.0	31.5
Can't choose	3.8	5.4	3.1	1.5	4.9	3.8
Not answered	0.6	0.7	0.3	0.5	0.7	0.6
Total frequency	156	542	358	412	288	1,756

Source: British Social Attitudes Survey (2001)

How do HR managers help firms to harness the richness of experience implied by generational diversity in a way that adds to firm performance?

The implications from the diversity literature that has investigated aspects of the business case would suggest that having a workforce that can 'empathise' with all sections of an increasingly diverse consumer base (often voiced as improving innovation) is an important consideration. In some ways this reflects the marketing model of generational distinctions.

Also, it is generally accepted that on-the-job training is an important element of individuals' human capital accumulation over their lifetime and that this process can often be characterised by a transfer of skills and abilities from older to younger workers (Eguchi 2004). However, studies that attempt to place a value on this process tend to be inconclusive (Eguchi 2004; Lindh 2005). One can view this intergenerational transfer as a positive aspect of age diversity.

If this intergenerational transfer is taking place, then older workers are acting to boost or supplement the productivity of younger workers, while incurring an opportunity cost in foregoing improvements to their own productivity. This observation may help to explain why an employee's productivity tends to be lower than their wage in later years – though many other explanations have been put forward (starting with Lazear 1979).

The Bank of Cyprus is one organisation that has successfully bridged the generation gap through the use of a number of principles (Schizas 1999). These principles are:

- Create an atmosphere of fellowship where people can learn from and with each other.
- Put the right people in the right jobs and avoid giving the young and talented jobs with little growth potential.
- Train line managers in supporting and facilitating rather than exercising oversight and control.
- Rotate people's positions so they can enrich their experiences and understand the needs of other people and departments.
- Provide training and development opportunities to all categories of worker to help them grow and maintain loyalty.
- Use the results of fair and generally accepted appraisal methods to support HR policies and decisions.
- Keep open communication channels, having an open-door approach and being responsive to employee needs.

Survey research from the Society for Human Resource Management (Burke 2004) also examined the success of a number of approaches to managing an intergenerational workforce (see Table 11).

Table 11: Approaches to managing an intergenerational workforce and the proportion of respondents finding each method very or moderately successful (Burke 2004)

	Very or moderately successful (%)
communicating information in multiple ways (that is, via email and during meetings)	94
collaborative discussion, decision-making or problem-solving	86
training managers in dealing with generational differences	77
team-building activities	78
offering different types of training	76
creating mentoring programmes to encourage workers of different generations to work together and share experiences	64
training employees on working with people of diverse age groups	69
conducting a demographic audit of the workplace to increase awareness of generational issues	43
mediation	34
keeping workers of different generations from being assigned to work together, where possible	5

This research suggests that the most successful way of addressing generational differences is through effective communication. Specifically, organisations should communicate messages in more than one way because employees from different generations prefer different methods of communicating. Collaborative decision-making and training managers to handle generational differences were also seen as relatively successful. Separating employees of different generations was seen as the least successful method.

CONCLUSIONS AND RECOMMENDATIONS

10

- **Much of the evidence that seems to support the existence of substantial generational differences is deeply flawed and should not be relied upon.**
- **Of that evidence which seems to have some validity, there is a tendency for the findings to reject the existence of generational cohorts as homogeneous groups and substantial divisions in behaviours and expectations between the various generations.**

Having issued this 'health warning', as we suggest in the initial stages of the report, isolating generational differences is particularly tricky. From a methodological standpoint, both those studies that accept and those that reject the claims for generational diversity cannot be seen as definitive. It is quite possible that any findings are being driven by age differences (if we adopt the approach of asking different generations at one point in time) and a variety of additional socioeconomic factors that are quite possibly transient.

So what can we take from the present study if the empirical evidence is at best mixed? There are a number of aspects of generational difference that seem to have some basis in fact and, while the empirical evidence is mixed, we do draw a number of broad conclusions in the areas of HR practice that employers can consider. Some of the areas where difference between employees seems apparent are:

- The increasing use of information and communications technologies is a clear and distinct dividing line between the generations. However, the major dividing line is probably between the generation that entered the labour market before 1985–1990 and the generations that entered after this period, although differences in the type of technology that employees are familiar with may also differ after this time. This dividing line has implications for a number of areas of HR practice.
- With respect to flexible working, it would seem that gender and age are more important in defining difference. While there is a possible generational effect here, it is that employers may eventually find that for the younger generations (X and Y) there is less and less need to consider flexible working as something that is split along gender lines, as more men take up flexible working at certain points in their working life; and women who have children face a greater variety of choices.
- An emphasis on diversity is more important for younger employees. In a recent survey by the Milkround (2007), a majority of respondents stated that they would be unwilling to work for employers who were not strong on diversity. Awareness of diversity issues is in itself an aspect that defines difference between the generations. Changes to employment law and globalisation are likely to have affected the way generations are treated and also interact with each other. It is therefore the concept of diversity itself, or the embracing and understanding of it, that might be one of the defining characteristics between generations.

While there may be both similarities and differences between generations, the important lesson from this discussion is that employers need to recognise that their employees will have a range of different needs and values. It is therefore necessary to treat employees as individuals as far as is possible. Consideration of diversity across a variety of characteristics is an important component of policies and practices that support the attainment of this goal. However, in considering diversity, we group people according to certain characteristics. It is important to recognise the potential danger that this approach can result in categorising or even stereotyping – we feel that some of the generational literature risks straying into such territory.

Ideally, we would sit down with each individual and put together a bespoke employment package that fully accommodates their diversity of needs. In reality we are forced to consider dimensions of diversity as a half-way house towards such a bespoke approach. In doing so, we must be careful that we do not spuriously add more dimensions than is strictly necessary. In the case set out here, distinguishing four generations simply does not seem to be needed in the majority of cases. We can add significantly to our understanding by just considering some of the major faultlines within the last 50 years that are likely to determine generational differences.

As with existing aspects of diversity, individuals are more or less determined by particular aspects of their characteristics in differing situations, and we may expect the same from different generations. For instance, when I am attempting to learn a new piece of software I may have more in common with somebody who is older than me (perhaps placing me in the Veteran or Boomer generations). In contrast, when looking into performance management, the opposite may apply and I may be more of a Generation Xer or a Yer. What we need to do is be aware of difference, rather than attempting to pigeon-hole into generational categories.

To date, despite the attention that has been given to generational differences in the industry press, it appears that organisations are doing very little to address the possible differences between these cohorts. For instance, recent research by the CIPD and London Business School (CIPD 2008c) found that relatively few of their respondents had made substantial changes to their policies and practices to address the potentially different needs of Generation Y. This was despite the fact that a high proportion of respondents saw this as important.

The CIPD and Penna report offers a 'top ten tips' to help organisation review and implement changes in their strategy and practice for generational diversity.

1. Analyse your workforce profile in terms of age and analyse the future impact of the changing generational mix.
2. Carry out an employee survey and analyse the views and motivations of different age groups. Ensure the survey captures views on respect and dignity in the workplace.
3. Audit your internal communications to assess whether your communications channels and styles are sufficiently flexible to meet the preferences of all groups of employees.
4. Does your employer brand really convey what is compelling about your organisation as a place to work in a way that attracts and engages all generations?
5. Rigorously analyse career development opportunities for all staff through stats and career conversations. Are any groups disadvantaged?
6. Flexibility: don't just meet legal requirements; consider radical changes to flexible working practices. Talk to staff. What would make a big difference to them could enhance your business.
7. Maximise opportunities to enhance coaching and mentoring across the generational groups. Use the experience of Veterans more effectively.
8. Re-engage Baby Boomers. Look at the impact of disengaged Baby Boomers in customer service or other business-critical roles. Re-engage them by ensuring that they are feeling challenged and have development opportunities.
9. Re-evaluate your corporate social responsibility (CSR) policies and practices. Who are they aimed at and who shows the most interest and engagement?
10. Identify the areas of commonality and build on them.

This report has provided an understanding of the different values and needs that exist among employees and some of the potential differences and similarities between these. What remains to be proven is whether these are due to generational cohort or to something else, such as age or life stage. The main lesson for employers should be that each employee is an individual who will not have the same needs and values as the next employee. Employers therefore need to take this into account when examining their management practices, employee development provision, recruitment practices and rewards structure. A 'pick and mix' approach to some of these may be the best approach to satisfy everyone's needs. In essence, employers need to find a balance in their people management practices that allows them to treat people as individuals while still being fair for all employees.

REFERENCES

ANSOORIAN, A., GOOD, P. and SAMUELSON, D. (2003) Managing generational differences. *Leadership*. May/June. pp34–36.

ARTHUR, M.B. and ROUSSEAU, D.M. (1996) The boundaryless career as a new employment principle. In: ARTHUR, M.B. and ROUSSEAU, D.M. (eds). *The boundaryless career*. New York: Oxford University Press. pp3–20.

BERL, P. (2006) Crossing the generational divide: supporting generational differences at work. *Exchange*. March/April. pp73–78.

BERRY, M. (2008) Generation Y: the hard facts. *Personnel Today*. 16 September. pp26–27.

BLUNDELL, R., MEGHIR, C. and SMITH, S. (2002) Pension incentives and the pattern of early retirement. *Economic Journal*. Vol 112, No 478, March. ppC153–C170.

BOVA, B. and KROTH, M. (2001) Workplace learning and Generation X. *Journal of Workplace Learning*. Vol 13, No 2. pp57–65

BOVA, B. and KROTH, M. (1999) Closing the gap: the mentoring of Generation X. *MPAEA Journal of Adult Education*. Summer. pp7–17.

BURKE, M. (2004) *Generational differences: survey report*. Alexandria, VA: Society for Human Resource Management.

CARD, D. and DINARDO, J. (2002) *Skill biased technological change and rising wage inequality: some problems and puzzles*. Working Paper No. W8769. Cambridge, Mass.: National Bureau of Economic Research (NBER).

CARLSON, H. (2004) Changing of the guard: a new generation of teacher leaders will raise quality-of-life priorities. *The School Administrator*. August.

CAUDRON, S. (1997) Can Generation Xers be trained? *Training and Development*. Vol 51, No 3, March. pp20–24.

CHARRIER, K. (2000) Marketing strategies for attracting and retaining Generation X police officers. *The Police Chief*. Vol 67, No 12, December. pp45–51.

CHARTERED INSTITUTE OF PERSONNEL AND DEVELOPMENT. (2009) *Labour Market Outlook: quarterly survey report Winter 2008/09 [online]*. London: CIPD. Available at: http://www.cipd.co.uk/subjects/hrpract/hrtrends/_qtrends.htm [Accessed 13 February 2009].

CHARTERED INSTITUTE OF PERSONNEL AND DEVELOPMENT. (2008a) *Innovation in the workplace: how are organisations responding to Generation Y employees and Web 2.0 technologies?* London: CIPD.

CHARTERED INSTITUTE OF PERSONNEL AND DEVELOPMENT. (2008b) *Managing an ageing workforce: the role of total reward*. London: CIPD.

CHARTERED INSTITUTE OF PERSONNEL AND DEVELOPMENT. (2008c) *Managing diversity and the business case*. Research into Practice report. London: CIPD.

CHARTERED INSTITUTE OF PERSONNEL AND DEVELOPMENT. (2008d) *Who learns at work? Employees' experiences of workplace learning*. London: CIPD.

CHARTERED INSTITUTE OF PERSONNEL AND DEVELOPMENT. (2003) *Who trains at work?* London: CIPD.

CHARTERED INSTITUTE OF PERSONNEL AND DEVELOPMENT. (2002) *Recruitment and retention*. Annual survey report. London: CIPD.

CORLEY, T. (1999). Becoming an employer of choice for Generation X: the elements of the deal. *Journal of Career Planning and Employment*. Vol 59, No 4, Summer. pp21–26.

CRANFIELD SCHOOL OF MANAGEMENT. (2007) *Recruitment Confidence Index*. Available at: http://www.rcisurvey.co.uk

CRUMPACKER, M. and CRUMPACKER, J. (2007) Succession planning and generational stereotypes: should HR consider age-based values and attitudes a relevant factor or a passing fad? *Public Personnel Management*. Vol 36, No 4, Winter. pp349–369.

DANIEL, K. and HEYWOOD, J.S. (2007) The determinants of hiring older workers: UK evidence. *Labour Economics*. Vol 14, No 1, January. pp35–51.

DENCKER, J., JOSHI, A. and MARTOCCHIO, J. (2007) Towards a theoretical framework linking generational memories to workplace attitudes and behaviours. *Human Resource Management Review.* Vol 18, No 3. pp180–187.

DEPARTMENT FOR TRADE AND INDUSTRY. (2004) *Business case for diversity and equality*. London: DTI, Women and Equality Unit.

DILWORTH and KINGSBURY (2005) Home to job spillover for Generation X, Boomers and Matures: a comparison. *Journal of Family and Economic Issues*. Vol 26, No 2. pp267–281.

DISNEY, R. (1999) Why have older men stopped working? In: GREGG, P. and WADSWORTH, J. (eds). *The state of working Britain*. Manchester: Manchester University Press.

DISNEY, R. and TANNER, S. (1999) *What can we learn from retirement expectations data?* London: Institute of Fiscal Studies.

EGUCHI, K. (2004) Trainers' dilemma of choosing between training and promotion. *Labour Economics*. Vol 11. pp765–783.

ETTINGTON, D.R. (1997) How human resource practices can help plateaued managers succeed. *Human Resource Management*. Vol 36, No 2, Summer. pp221–234.

FERRIS, G. and KING, T. (1992) The politics of age discrimination in organizations. *Journal of Business Ethics*. Vol 11, No 5/6. pp341–350.

FILIPCZAK, B. (1994) It's just a job: Generation X at work. *Training*. Vol 31, No 4, April. pp21–27.

FINKELSTEIN, L.M. and BURKE, M.J. (1998) Age stereotyping at work: the role of rater and contextual factors on evaluations of job applicants. *Journal of General Psychology*. Vol 125, No 4, October. pp317–345.

FOSTER, C. and HARRIS, L. (2005) Easy to say, difficult to do: diversity management in retail. *Human Resource Management Journal*. Vol 15, No 3. pp4–17.

GIANCOLA, F. (2006) The generation gap: more myth than reality. *Human Resource Planning*. Vol 29, No 4. pp32–37.

GLASS, A. (2007) Understanding generational differences for competitive success. *Industrial and Commercial Training*. Vol 39, No 2. pp98–103.

GONZALES, C. (2006) *A causal comparative study of work ethic as a function of generational cohorts*. [PhD thesis], University of Phoenix.

HESSEN, C. and LEWIS, B. (2001) Steps you can take to hire, keep and inspire Generation Xers. *Leadership and Management in Engineering*. Vol 1, No 1. pp42–44.

JENKINS, J. (2008) Strategies for managing talent in a multigenerational workforce. *Employment Relations Today*. Vol 34, No 4, Winter. pp19–26.

JURKIEWICZ, C. (2000) Generation X and the public employee. *Public Personnel Management*. Vol 29, No 1, Spring. pp55–74

JURKIEWICZ, C. and BROWN, R. (1998) GenXers vs. Boomers vs. Matures: generational comparisons of public employees' motivation. *Review of Public Personnel Administration*. Vol 18, No 4, Fall. pp18–37.

KARP, H. and SIRIAS, D. (2001) Generational conflict: a new paradigm for teams of the 21st century. *Gestalt Review*. Vol 5, No 2. pp71–87.

KELLIHER, C. and ANDERSON, D. (2008) *Flexible working and performance*. Cranfield: Cranfield School of Management.

LAZEAR, E.P. (1979) Why is there mandatory retirement? *Journal of Political Economy*. Vol 87, December. pp1261–1284.

LINDH, T. (2005) *Productivity consequences at the plant level of workforce ageing – stagnation or a Horndal effect?* XIX Annual Conference of the European Society for Population Economics, Paris.

LITVIN, D. (1997) The discourse of diversity: from biology to management. *Organization*. Vol 4, No 2. pp187–209.

LORETTO, W. and WHITE, P. (2006) Employers' attitudes, practices and policies towards older workers. *Human Resource Management Journal.* Vol 16, No 3. pp313–330.

LOSYK, B. (1997) How to manage an X'er. *The Futurist*. Vol 31, No 2, March/April. p43.

MACLEOD, A. (2008). *Generation Y: unlocking the talent of young managers.* London: Chartered Management Institute.

MCCAFFERTY, F. (2003) The challenge of selecting tomorrow's police officers from Generations X and Y. *Journal of the American Academy of Psychiatry and the Law*. Vol 31, No 1, March. pp78–88.

MCDONALD, K. and HITE, L. (2008) The next generation of career success: implications for HRD. *Advances in Developing Human Resources*. Vol 10, No 1, February. pp86–103.

MCNAIR, S., FLYNN, M. and OWEN, L. (2004) *Changing work in later life: a study of job transitions.* Guildford: University of Surrey. Centre for Research into the Older Workforce.

MICHIELSENS, E., BINGHAM, C. and CLARKE, L. (2008) *Implementing diversity employment policies: examples from large London companies*. London: London First and University of Westminster. Westminster Business School.

MILKROUND. (2007) *Supporting diversity and equal opportunities for graduates*. London: Diversity Milkround.

MOEN, P. (2005) Beyond the career mystique: 'time in', 'time out', and 'second acts'. *Sociological Forum*. Vol 20, No 2, June. pp189–208.

NELSON, A., NEMEC, K., SOLVIK and RAMSDEN, C. (2004) *The evaluation of the Work–Life Balance Challenge Fund*. London: Department for Trade and Industry.

NG, T. and FELDMAN, D. (2007) Organizational embeddedness and occupational embeddedness across career stages. *Journal of Vocational Behavior*. Vol 70. pp336–351.

O'BANNON, G. (2001) Managing our future: the Generation X factor. *Public Personnel Management*. Vol 30, No 1, Spring. pp95–109.

POLACH, J. (2006) *Working with Veterans, Boomers, Xers, Ys: It's about their age, not when they were born*. St Louis Park, Minn.: Leadership Solutions. Working paper. Available at: http://www.lsi-mn.com/assorted/generations.pdf [Accessed 13 February 2009].

POWELL, G.N. and MAINIERO, L.A. (1992) Cross-currents in the river of time: conceptualizing the complexities of women's careers. *Journal of Management*. Vol 18, No 2, June. pp215–237.

REDMAN, T. and SNAPE, E. (2002) Ageism in teaching: stereotypical beliefs and discriminatory attitudes towards the over-50s. *Work, Employment and Society*. Vol 16, No 2. pp355–371.

RICHARDS, S. (2003) *The interactive syllabus: a resource-based, constructivist approach to learning*. Lansing, Mich.: The Michigan Virtual University.

ROBERTS, B.W. and FRIEND, W. (1998) Career momentum in midlife women: life context, identity, and personality correlates. *Journal of Occupational Health Psychology*. Vol 3, No 3, July. pp195–208.

RUCH, W. (2000) How to keep Gen X employees from becoming x-employees. *Training & Development*. Vol 54, No 4, April. pp40–43.

RUPP, D.E., VODANOVICH, S.J. and CREDÉ, M. (2005) The multidimensional nature of ageism: construct validity and group differences. *Journal of Social Psychology*. Vol 145, No 3, June. pp335–362.

SALMON, G. (2004) *E-moderating: the key to teaching and learning online*. London: RoutledgeFalmer.

SCHANK, R. (2005) *Lessons in learning, e-learning, and training: reflections and perspectives for the bewildered trainer*. Chichester: Pfeiffer Wiley.

SCHIZAS, C. (1999) Capitalizing on a generation gap. *Management Review*. Vol 88, No 6. pp62–68.

SMITH, W.S. (2008) *Decoding generational differences: fact, fiction . . .or should we just get back to work?* Deloitte Development LLC. Available at: http://www.deloitte.com/dtt/cda/doc/content/us_Talent_DecodingGenerationalDifferences.pdf [Accessed 13 February 2009].

STURGES, J. (1999) What it means to succeed: personal conceptions of career success held by male and female managers at different ages. *British Journal of Management*. Vol 10, No 3, September. pp239–252.

SUBELIANI, D. and TSOGAS, G. (2005) Managing diversity in the Netherlands: a case study of Rabobank. *International Journal of Human Resource Management*. Vol 16, No 5. pp831–851.

SULLIVAN, S.E., CARDEN, W.A. and MARTIN, D.F. (1998) Careers in the next millennium: directions for future research. *Human Resource Management Review*. Vol 8, No 2, Summer. pp165–185.

SWANN, W.B. Jr., POLZER, J.T., SEYLE, C. and KO, S. (2004) Finding value in diversity: verification of personal and social self-views in diverse groups. *Academy of Management Review*. Vol 29. pp9–27.

TAYLOR, M. (2005) Generation NeXt: today's postmodern student – meeting, teaching, and serving. Collection of papers on self-study and institutional improvement. *The Higher Learning Commission*. Vol 2. pp99–107. Chicago: The Higher Learning Commission.

TAYLOR, P. and WALKER, A. (2003) Age discrimination in the labour market and policy responses: the situation in the United Kingdom. *The Geneva Papers on Risk and Insurance*. Vol 28, No 4. pp612–624.

TAYLOR, P.E. and URWIN, P. (2001) Age and participation in vocational education and training. *Work, Employment and Society*. Vol 15, No 4. pp763–779.

TAYLOR, P.E. and URWIN, P. (1999) Recent trends in the labour force participation of older people in the UK. *The Geneva Papers on Risk and Insurance*. Vol 24, No 4, October. pp551–579.

TERJESEN, S., VINNICOMBE, S. and FREEMAN, C. (2007) Attracting Generation Y graduates: organisational attributes, likelihood to apply and sex differences. *Career Development International*. Vol 12, No 6. pp504–522.

TULGAN, B. (1997) Generation X: slackers? Or the workforce of the future? *Employment Relations Today*. Vol 24, No 2, Summer. pp55–64.

TULGAN, B. (1996) *Managing Generation X: how to bring out the best in young talent*. Oxford: Capstone.

TURNER COMMISSION. (2004) *First report – evidence*. London: The Stationery Office.

URWIN, P. (2004) *Age matters: a review of existing survey evidence.* Department of Trade and Industry, Employment Relations Research Series, No 24. London: The Stationery Office.

URWIN, P., BLANDEN, J., BUSCHA, F. and STURGIS, P. (2009, forthcoming) *The effect of adult education on intra-generational social mobility: evidence from longitudinal data in the United Kingdom.* London: Department for Innovation, Universities and Skills.

URWIN, P., MICHIELSENS, E. and WATERS, J. (2006) The contribution of employee relations practice to high performance workplaces: case studies on work–life balance and diversity practice. CIPD Professional Standards Conference, Keele University, June; also presented at 2006 BUIRA Conference.

WHITE, M., HILL, S., MILLS, C. and SMEATON, D. (2004) *Managing to change? British workplaces and the future of work*. Basingstoke: Palgrave Macmillan.

ZEMKE, R., RAINES, C. and FILIPCZAK, B. (2000) *Generations at work: managing the clash of Veterans, Boomers, Xers and Nexters in your workplace*. New York: Amacom.